GRATINS

GRATINS

Savory *and* Sweet Recipes
from Oven *to* Table

Text and Recipes by
TINA SALTER

Photographs by
PAUL MOORE

Produced by
CATHERINE JACOBES

TEN SPEED PRESS
Berkeley | Toronto

TEN SPEED PRESS
Box 7123
Berkeley, California 94707
www.tenspeed.com

Distributed in Australia by Simon and Schuster Australia,
in Canada by Ten Speed Press Canada, in New Zealand by
Southern Publishers Group, in South Africa by Real Books,
and in the United Kingdom and Europe by Airlift Book
Company. .

Design by **Catherine Jacobes Design**
Food styling by **George Dolese**
Food styling assistance by **Elisabet der Nederlanden**
Prop styling by **Paul Moore and George Dolese**
Photography assistance by **Jeff McLain**

Library of Congress Cataloging-in-Publication Data

Salter, Tina.
  Savory and sweet recipes from oven to table / Tina Salter
and Catherine Jacobes.
      p. cm.
  Includes index.
  ISBN-10: 1-58008-623-3
  ISBN-13: 978-1-58008-623-3
  1. Cookery, French. I. Jacobes, Catherine. II. Title.
  TX719.S336 2004
  641.5944--dc22

                              2004009715

First printing 2004
Printed in Korea

2 3 4 5 6 7 8 9 10 — 08 07 06 05

For Rhiannon and Ian—
More than every blade of grass

CONTENTS

ACKNOWLEDGMENTS

Beginning a new project is always a daunting task, but working on gratins has been such fun. Gratins offer the opportunity of experimenting with flavors, and because they are so quick to assemble, you can pop one in the oven while researching others. None of this would have been possible, however, without the hands, palates, and collaboration of many friends.

First and foremost, special thanks to *le Gratin* of book designers Catherine Jacobes, whose vision, encouragement, and support instigated this book and whose creative art direction always benefits any project. The warm, creamy interior is the substance of any great gratin, and my colleague Christine Swett continues to be the substantive friend, tester, taster, and recipe writer who makes sense of my notes. Thank you both.

Photography plays a crucial part in any cookbook, and Paul Moore completely captured the crusty appeal of gratins. All the shots were beautifully styled and propped by the extraordinarily talented George Dolese. Thank you both. Thank you also to Jeff McLain and Elizabet der Nerderlanden, their hardworking and trusty assistants.

Thanks must also be given to my friendly tasters and testers: Shirlene Brass, who joined me for a cup of tea when taste buds were overwhelmed; Brian and Sibeal Whitty, Sharon Doyle, and Mimi Little, who came at all hours to taste and "suggest"; and my two assistants, Rhiannon and Ian, who continue to eat gratins daily.

Thanks to Steve Siegelman, who was always available with advice and direction; he is an invaluable support on any project. And to our erudite copy editors, Carrie Bradley, and Jasmine Star who painstakingly worked, sometimes through the night, to check, review, and clarify.

Finally, thanks to those at Ten Speed Press, especially Lorena Jones, whose editoral expertise, support, and encouragement from the very beginning are valued and appreciated beyond belief; Annie Nelson, whose patience, direction, and exacting standards guided us; and Phil Wood and Kirsty Melville, who, in their position at the helm, inspire and motivate us all.

INTRODUCTION

Gratins—baked dishes with a rich, creamy interior and a crisp, golden topping—have been around for centuries. In France, the term has even taken on metaphorical meaning: the aristocracy is often referred to as *le gratin*, much as we would talk about the "upper crust."

Indeed, it is the crust that makes a gratin. As the ingredients below it meld and soften, a gratin's topping—often made with toasted bread crumbs, nuts, cheese, or a combination—becomes mouthwateringly browned and crunchy from the intense heat of the oven or broiler. It's that contrast of creamy and crisp in every bite that makes a gratin so irresistible.

A gratin can be sweet or savory, elegant or homespun, a supporting player or the star of a meal. It can be as sophisticated as the classic *Gratin Dauphinoise*, which turns potatoes into a dish worthy of a prince, or take the form of an elegant appetizer of individual artichoke crowns topped with crabmeat and gratinéed under the broiler. It can be as simple as vegetables topped with herbed bread crumbs, or ripe strawberries under a golden puff of lightly browned custard sauce. All the gratinéed dishes in this book have the traditional crisp crust. Some just use the traditional ingredient of cream, cooked to caramelize into the crust. Others use bread crumbs seasoned with herbs and sometimes garlic and moistened with olive oil or butter. Some have added nuts, seeds, or even crushed tortilla chips. Some use cheese, either alone or in combination with other ingredients. Use your imagination and the recipes provided to create your own versions. Just remember that the crisp crust should top a deliciously, meltingly moist interior.

Each of these recipes has been tested and approved by family and friends. Together they make for a fine repertoire of gratins, but I also hope that this book will inspire you to create gratins with flavor and texture combinations of your own imagination. A stop at the farm stand or a trip to the grocery store might present you with some seasonal fruits and vegetables too good to resist. Take them home and start creating. Just think about their texture and water and starch content, then work out if they need to be blanched, sautéed, or otherwise cooked before topping. Remember that all vegetables vary in the time they take to soften or in the amount of stock or cream that they absorb; be prepared to use your judgment and cook a little longer if necessary, perhaps adding a little more stock or cream. This rule applies to any recipe in this book. Don't be afraid of adding other vegetables to a dish, and use the new expertise you will acquire to improvise. If you have leftover cooked vegetables, they can be moistened with a little stock or cream and topped with buttered bread crumbs or cheese to make a delicious gratin in themselves.

No matter how you prepare it or what you put in, a good gratin always produces the same result. When it's placed on the table, its golden crust is resplendent, promising a rich, tempting filling just below the surface, and people can't help themselves. "Ahhhs" of anticipation are the usual effect. Truly the "upper crust" of casseroles, a gratin is much more than just a satisfying hot dish; it's a wonderful way to put love on the table. I hope you and the people you love enjoy these recipes as much as I do.

GRATIN COOKING BASICS

Equipment

Although the recipes in this book are simple and straightforward, the following section offers some tips about tools for gratin making, along with a review of other basic kitchen equipment employed.

GRATIN DISHES

There aren't many tools necessary to make a gratin, but it's hard to make a gratin unless you have the right dish. Remember, it's often the dish itself that gives gratin recipes their name.

Gratin dishes are specially designed to be wide and shallow to afford a large surface area that promotes the crisp crust indicative of a gratin. A gratin dish is never more than 2 inches deep. It can be oval, square, rectangular, or round. It may be made of metal, ceramic, terra-cotta, porcelain, or glass. Gratin dishes should always be oven and broiler safe.

Gratin dishes range in appearance, from plain and simple glass to elaborately decorated clay. Equip yourself with two or three in different shapes and sizes to fit most of the recipes in this book. Gratin dishes are also good for roasting and for custards and puddings, and they make great serving pieces, too. I find myself using the traditional oval gratin most often. Sets of three nested together are easy to find, usually in sizes of 8, 10, and 12 inches (3 cups to $1^1/2$ quarts). A 12-inch stainless steel-lined or copper gratin dish is a versatile choice, as you can use it to cook on the stove top, as well. Other popular sizes are the 7 by 9-inch (1-quart) rectangle; 9-inch (1-quart) square; 8 by 10-inch ($1^1/2$-quart) rectangle, and 8 by 11-inch (2-quart) rectangle.

In a pinch you can use some of the standard baking pans, pie plates, ramekins, or custard cups you may already have in your cupboard. Just make sure that they are oven and broiler safe and that they aren't too deep—again, no more than 2 inches. To ensure that you choose a dish of appropriate size, I have given both the length and the quart measure for the baking dish for each recipe. Square and rectangular gratins are measured across the width and length, in inches, with a quart measure for volume. Ovals are measured across their widest point, also with a quart measure for volume.

Every brand varies, so if the exact size is not available, err on a slightly larger size, to prevent spillage. If you choose to substitute individual gratin dishes, remember to adjust the cooking time accordingly; check for doneness 10 minutes and again 5 minutes before the stated cooking time for one larger dish.

BAKING SHEETS

Always set the gratin dish on a sturdy baking sheet with a rim to aid transport from counter to oven, for stability, and to catch any drips. These are available in aluminum, stainless steel, and nonstick versions. Lighter-weight baking sheets tend to warp or twist upon heating, giving the gratin dish an uneven base and often causing it to brown unevenly or spill. To make cleanup even easier, line the baking sheet with aluminum foil.

OVEN AND BROILER

For baking gratins, place the oven rack in the center position and preheat for at least 20 minutes. It is wise to check the oven temperature with an oven thermometer.

If the gratin is hot and bubbly but the top has failed to brown, you can transfer it to the broiler for 2 or 3 minutes. Broil until golden,

but watch carefully—the surface can change from brown to black in seconds.

To broil a gratin, adjust the oven rack or broiler pan so that the top surface of the gratin will be about 4 inches from the heat source. Preheat the broiler for at least 10 minutes. Leave the oven or broiler door ajar; this not only enables you to check the color to prevent burning, but also allows the air to circulate.

KITCHEN BUTANE TORCH

Small kitchen butane blowtorches, available in cookware stores, can be used in the final browning of some dishes. They are especially efficient at caramelizing sugar on the surface of desserts as they give the user complete control in directing the heat without heating up the custard in the dish below.

OVEN MITTS

Working with the oven and broiler to manage trays of bubbling hot gratins requires protection from the heat. Good-quality oven mitts protect hands and wrists more than a simple pot holder or folded towel can.

KNIVES AND VEGETABLE PEELERS

Sharp knives are one of the basic tools required in any kitchen. Sharp knives are safer; it takes less pressure to slice through foods, thus reducing the risk of slippage and accidents. To maintain a sharp edge, knives should be professionally sharpened every year or so, and the edge should be freshened with a sharpening steel at home before each use.

MANDOLINE

A mandoline, a flat, rectangular slicing tool, is a great aid for slicing foods quickly, thinly, and uniformly—a preparation commonly called for in a fast-cooking, attractive gratin. Mandolines are especially efficient for slicing root vegetables. Small, compact, plastic models are available as alternatives to the large, stainless steel, adjustable versions, usually French, with folding legs. Either type is a great addition to the kitchen arsenal. Always use the guard to protect fingers and knuckles from the very sharp blade.

FOOD PROCESSORS AND BLENDERS

Although it's only been around for about thirty years, the food processor is a necessity in modern kitchens. It is especially efficient for making the fresh bread crumbs for gratins. Cut bread into cubes before adding to the processor. A blender is an alternative to the food processor for making bread crumbs, though not as efficient, as it only produces good crumbs in small batches at a time.

GRATERS, RASPS, AND ZESTERS

There are a number of good options for creating the finely crumbed ingredients for topping a gratin. A box grater made of stainless steel, with sides offering different-sized perforations, is the classic and versatile kitchen workhorse used for grating cheese and other ingredients. Newly popular and widely available kitchen rasps, based on the carpenter's design, offer a very efficient alternative to the traditional box grater, with numerous razor-sharp blades on a long, narrow plane to create finely shredded citrus zest or fine, fluffy gratings of hard cheeses. A zester is a small, handheld tool with a thin row of tiny perforations specifically designed for removing the zest from citrus fruits. They work well for making long strips of zest that can then be chopped finely, if desired.

BASIC PANS

Every cook works more happily with a set of good-quality pans. A basic inventory ideally contains three saucepans of various sizes (1, 2, and 3 quarts), a stockpot or large soup pot, a sauté pan, and a skillet. Good cooking pans are heavy-duty, with a core of aluminum or copper for efficient heat conduction.

Basic Ingredients

Because the ingredients in a gratin are often few and simple, it is important that they be of the best quality. Vegetables should be ripe, fresh, and seasonal; milk and cream should be the best that you can find. Where possible, cheese should be from the farm. Shop at stores with a good turnover to ensure freshness. Small stores with a knowledgeable staff often give samples for you to taste before you buy. This gives you the opportunity to learn new flavors and to be creative. Maybe there is a cheese or ham that would work instead of my recipe suggestion. Try it and see!

CREAM AND MILK

Cream is an important component of many of the gratins in this book. From the sumptuous Gratin Dauphinoise (page 54), or scalloped potatoes, to the moist Corn, Tomato, and Basil Gratin (page 37), cream adds a soft, silky texture and forms the crisp golden crust of the traditional gratin. Use heavy cream (with a butterfat content of 36 to 40 percent) when called for in a recipe. Unlike half-and-half, heavy cream is very stable when heated and unlikely to curdle. If you want to lighten a dish, you can substitute a little milk for the total amount of cream, but not more than 30 percent of the total or you run the risk of it curdling. The wonderful texture and full rich flavor that cream imparts to a gratin is worth the calories—since a cup or two serves 4 to 6 people, a single portion isn't too sinful.

CRÈME FRAÎCHE AND SOUR CREAM

Crème fraîche and sour cream are what's known as "cultured creams". Crème fraîche has a similar flavor to sour cream but a higher butterfat content, so it doesn't curdle when heated. Crème fraîche needs to be thinned a bit before adding to a recipe, otherwise it will thicken to the consistency of cream cheese when subjected to long, slow cooking. Add 2 or 3 tablespoons of milk or stock per cup until you achieve the consistency of heavy cream. You can usually find crème fraîche at well-stocked supermarkets or specialty foods stores, but if you can't or you prefer, you can easily make it at home:

In a small bowl, combine 1 cup heavy cream with 2 tablespoons buttermilk. Mix well and let stand, covered, at room temperature until it thickens, about 12 hours. Refrigerate your homemade crème fraîche for up to 10 days.

Sour cream, with its lower butterfat content, often curdles. If you want to use sour cream in a recipe, you'll need to stabilize it with a little flour, as I did in the New Potato Gratin with Sour Cream, Chive, and Onion (page 62).

BUTTER

Unsalted butter allows control of the salt content in recipes. Its rich and creamy flavor adds an unctuous quality to gratins. Butter is used to grease pans in cream- and milk-based dishes for the same rich flavor qualities and to prevent sticking. Use generously for dishes requiring long, slow cooking. Butter also aids the browning of gratins and a little extra can always be added to the surface for a markedly golden top.

CHEESE

Gratins use cheese not only for flavor but also for the great melting and crisping qualities. Cheese is included in many of these gratin recipes, not only on the top, where it's baked or broiled to glorious golden crustiness, but also in sauces or layered between vegetables.

The ancient Greeks considered cheese a gift from the gods and savored its huge variety of flavors. Not much has changed in cheese cultures to this day. France alone is said to produce more than 350 varieties, one for every day of the year. Each cheese has it's own flavor, texture, and smell. It is generally made from cow, sheep, goat, or buffalo milk. It can range in age from young and fresh—no more than 1 to 6 weeks old, like mascarpone and ricotta—to hard, pressed, aged grana cheeses (those with a particular grainy texture such as Parmesan), aged for up to over 4 years. The cheeses used in the recipes in this book were chosen for both flavor and texture, exploiting the wide and wonderful variety but sticking to those that are readily available.

Parmesan, a hard grana grating cheese, is from Italy. Parmigiano-Reggiano, the king of grana cheese, is very expensive but worth the price in flavor and texture. It's made with unpasteurized cow's milk from the area around Parma and is produced every year between the first of April and the eleventh of November. The curds are cut into very small grains, then cooked, pressed, and aged for a minimum of 1 year and up to more than 4 years. There are other grana cheeses labeled as Parmesan that work well in recipes, but the price generally reflects the quality. I recommend buying the best you can find. And always buy in wedges and grate it yourself; never resort to the green box.

Pecorino Romano is a hard-pressed Italian cheese made from sheep's milk. It's flavor is much more gamey and a somewhat acidic than Parmesan. Taste before using, as some versions are quite salty and you may need to adjust the salt in your recipe accordingly.

Cheddar is a firm, pressed cheese readily available in most markets, but few resemble the flavor or texture of the farmhouse Cheddar from its original location in England. Good, flavorful Cheddar is also available from Canada, Ireland, and the United States. Use aged, sharp Cheddars for their full flavor. Avoid the processed imitations—they're just not the same.

Gruyère and Emmenthaler have a distinctive sweet, nutty flavor that melts beautifully. Produced in France and Switzerland, these two cheeses can be used alone or combined with other cheeses.

Fontina is a nutty cheese with a trace of honey flavor from the Val d'Aosta in the Italian Alps. Like Gruyère and Emmenthaler, fontina melts smoothly; but it can be expensive.

Mozzarella is a fresh cheese that has been pulled and shaped in hot water to make it smooth. Cheeses like mozzarella melt into creamy strings and lend luxurious surprise to a filling, like that in the Prosciutto–Mashed Potato Gratin (page 62).

Ricotta is fresh, granular cheese that is made from the whey of other cheeses. It is available in most markets in tubs. Stirred into polenta, it lightens the dish for a soft, creamy supper dish.

Feta was originally a Greek cheese made with goat and cow milk. Now fetas from France, Bulgaria, and the United States are readily available. Some are so mild as to be almost tasteless, while others are strong and salty. Taste before using. If it's too salty, soak it in milk for 10 minutes to remove some of the salt flavor. Drain and pat dry. Adjust the salt in the recipe accordingly.

Blue cheeses are many and varied, made with cow, goat or sheep milk. Some are mild, while others are strong enough to knock your socks off. They are all made with curds inoculated with a mold to encourage the bluing that flavors the cheese. Popular blue cheeses are Stilton, Gorgonzola, and Maytag blue.

Processed cheeses include other ingredients such as vegetable oils, butter, emulsifiers, artificial preservatives, and flavorings. Avoid these products.

BREAD CRUMBS

Bread crumbs are often a crucial ingredient in the toppings used to give the surface of a gratin its crunch. However, processed and supermarket breads lacks the texture and flavor needed for a good crumb and will just become doughy, while canned bread crumbs are an expensive, tasteless alternative. This book calls for only high-quality, fresh bread crumbs; some bakeries sell them, but it's easiest to make your own. In any case, use a coarse, country bread with a firm, chewy texture. It's a great way to use up leftovers: just freeze heels or odd slices in a plastic container or sealable plastic bag and grind as needed, or grind the crumbs first and store in the same way.

The question of whether or not to remove the crust on bread for bread crumbs is an ongoing issue. Because the bread crumbs in this book are generally used as the topping, where they will be toasted further in the oven or under the broiler, remove any dark, hard crusts and leave on the lighter, softer golden areas.

Use fresh bread crumbs that are a day or two old, depending on your preference; dried bread crumbs have a finer consistency.

Fresh bread crumbs: Fresh bread crumbs are still somewhat soft and uneven in size and shape, which adds a pleasant rustic look to the surface of a gratin. To make fresh bread crumbs, use any bread that's a day or two old, or dry bread slices on the countertop overnight. Tear the bread into large pieces and process in a food processor or blender to the desired texture.

Dried bread crumbs: For dried bread crumbs, use bread that has dried out, or dry in a 200°F oven for about 1 hour. Tear the bread into large pieces and process in a blender or food processor into fine crumbs, or grate the bread on the fine rasps of a handheld grater.

Toasted bread crumbs can be made by toasting slices of bread in a 350°F oven for 5 to 8 minutes; let cool and process in a blender or food processor. Because toasted bread is so crunchy, it can be sealed in a plastic bag and smashed into crumbs with a rolling pin. This process produces an attractive uneven-sized crumb. Bread crumbs can also be toasted with butter or oil in a skillet; you can substitute toasted breadcrumbs for fresh if the topping of a recipe is added at the last minute and requires a short cooking time.

Leftover oiled or buttered croutons (slices of bread brushed with butter or oil) make a great crust when they are made into crumbs; they can also be sealed in a plastic bag and smashed into crumbs with a rolling pin.

POTATOES

Potatoes are a tuber that is native to the Andes Mountains of South America. They were not introduced to Europe until the late sixteenth century or to North America until the early seventeenth century. There are now more than five thousand varieties produced worldwide.

Choose dry, firm potatoes that smell fresh—sprouts or green surfaces indicate bad storage or exposure to light and should be avoided (an alkaloid called "solanin" causes the color change and is toxic if consumed in quantity). Store potatoes in a cool, dry, dark place. Avoid the refrigerator, as this will cause the starch to convert to sugar and a change in color as the potatoes cook.

Many varieties of potato suitable for gratin making are readily available in supermarkets. Russet, or Idaho, potatoes are long ovals with brown, rough skin and a starchy, floury texture that makes them great for baking and for French fries. I use them in the Spinach,

Bacon, and Potato Gratin (page 51) and in the Prosciutto–Mashed Potato Gratin (page 58).

Waxier varieties, such as long whites and red-skinned potatoes, are lower in moisture and starch and have a waxy texture. Yukon golds, with a creamy yellow flesh, are a favorite of mine. Use them in some of the gratins where potatoes are combined with cream to really accentuate their rich flavor.

New potatoes are small, young potatoes. They can be any variety and are crisp and waxy in texture, with thin skins. Fingerling and other varieties of diminutive potatoes, though small with rich, creamy flavor, may not be young. Both new and fingerling potatoes are generally cooked whole in their skins; for those that seem mature enough to warrant peeling, it's best if they are steamed or boiled and drained first. The skins can then be removed with a small, sharp paring knife. Just make a small incision and pull the skins away; they should release easily in small strips.

STOCK

Homemade chicken or vegetable stock has a superior flavor and is always preferable to canned or concentrate. Making your own is easy, requiring a minimum of effort, and doing so gives complete control of the salt content. Stock can be made in large quantities and stored in sealable plastic bags in the freezer. If you substitute store-bought broth, use the low-sodium variety and taste before adding salt to a recipe.

CHICKEN STOCK

Makes 2 to 3 quarts Good homemade chicken stock is the foundation of many soups and sauces. It tastes much better than canned, and as no salt is added, it gives you complete control of the seasoning in any dish. Because it takes no more time to make a large batch than a small one, feel free to double the recipe and store the extra in measured containers in the freezer.

5 pounds chicken wings, backs, giblets, and other parts, rinsed

2 yellow onions, halved

2 carrots, scrubbed and cut into 4 chunks

2 celery stalks, cut into 4 chunks

1 bay leaf

10 black peppercorns

IN A LARGE STOCKPOT, COMBINE THE CHICKEN PARTS, onions, carrots, celery, bay leaf and peppercorns. Add enough cold water to cover by 1 inch. Bring to a boil over high heat, skimming off and discarding any foam as it rises to the top. Decrease the heat to medium-low and simmer for 2 to 3 hours.

STRAIN THE STOCK THROUGH A FINE-MESH SIEVE and discard the solids. Let cool to room temperature. Cover and refrigerate until cold; remove any congealed fat from the surface of the stock and discard.

THE STOCK CAN BE REFRIGERATED, covered, for up to 3 days or frozen, in airtight containers, for up to 3 months.

VEGETABLE STOCK

Makes 2 to 3 quarts The flavor of vegetable stock is entirely dependent on the vegetables that go into it. This recipe is for a very basic stock that can be used in a variety of dishes. Feel free to add other vegetables like mushrooms or corn cobs for a more distinctive flavor, but avoid cruciferous veggies like cabbage and broccoli——they will add a strong distinctive flavor that will overpower any dish.

2 medium yellow onions, halved

2 leeks, white and green parts, cleaned (see page 47) and cut into 2-inch lengths

2 carrots, scrubbed and cut into 4 chunks

2 celery stalks, cut into 4 chunks

2 cloves garlic, smashed

6 sprigs flat-leaf parsley

1 bay leaf

10 black peppercorns

IN A LARGE STOCKPOT, COMBINE THE ONIONS, leeks, carrots, celery, garlic, parsley, bay leaf, and peppercorns. Add enough cold water to cover by 1 inch. Bring to a boil over high heat, skimming off and discarding any foam as it rises to the top. Decrease the heat to medium-low and simmer for 2 hours.

STRAIN THE STOCK THROUGH A FINE-MESH SIEVE and discard the solids. Let the stock cool to room temperature, then; cover and refrigerate.

THE STOCK CAN BE REFRIGERATED, covered, for up to 3 days or frozen, in airtight containers, for up to 3 months.

FIRSTS *and* SMALL PLATES

GRATINÉED GRAPEFRUIT

Serves 4 to 6 Grapefruits are available year-round, but they reach their sweet and juicy best in midwinter, a boon during the long months when fresh fruit is scarce. This gratin is easy to make and a delicious surprise as a light first course; though a sweet dish, the tartness of the grapefruit is a perfect appetite awakener. Be sure to drain the grapefruit thoroughly, or the sugar will not caramelize. Use Demerara sugar—coarse, light brown crystals with a touch of added molasses—because it keeps its crunch, but washed raw or granulated sugar is a fine substitute.

4 large grapefruits

2 tablespoons dark rum (optional)

$^1/_4$ cup Demerara or other washed raw cane sugar

PREHEAT THE BROILER. Using a sharp knife, peel the grapefruit, taking care to remove all the white pith. Holding a grapefruit over a bowl, slice between the membrane and the fruit on each side of each segment, and let the freed segments drop into the bowl. Repeat with the remaining grapefruit. Squeeze the membranes over the bowl to release any remaining juice.

USING A SLOTTED SPOON, remove the segments from the juice and divide evenly among 4 individual ramekins or arrange in a $5^1/_2$ by $7^1/_2$-inch (2-cup) gratin dish. Drink the remaining juice or reserve for another use.

DRIZZLE THE RUM EVENLY OVER THE GRAPEFRUIT and sprinkle the sugar evenly over the top. Place the dish(es) on a sturdy baking sheet. Set under the broiler, about 4 inches from the heat source, and broil until the surface is golden and beginning to brown, 3 to 5 minutes. Serve immediately.

GRATINÉED FIGS *with* CHÈVRE

Serves 6 Figs have a short season, just a few weeks around the middle of July and then again for a precious week or two in September, so make the most of them while you can. This simple dish accentuates the figs' sweetness and counters it with the salty tang of fresh goat cheese. It's a perfect start to a summer meal or an impressive addition to an antipasto platter.

9 ripe fresh Black Mission figs

4 ounces chèvre or other soft fresh goat cheese

3 tablespoons dark brown sugar

12 very thin slices (about 4 ounces) prosciutto

6 small fresh fig leaves, for garnish

PREHEAT THE BROILER. Trim the stem and flower ends from the figs and halve lengthwise. Spread the cut surface of each fig half with about $^1/_2$ tablespoon of the cheese and sprinkle each with about $^1/_2$ teaspoon of the sugar. Place the figs $^1/_2$ inch apart in an 8 by 10-inch ($1^1/_2$-quart) gratin dish.

PLACE THE GRATIN DISH ON A STURDY BAKING SHEET. Set under the broiler, about 4 inches from the heat source, and broil until the sugar is golden and caramelized, 3 to 5 minutes.

ARRANGE 2 SLICES OF THE PROSCIUTTO and 3 fig halves on each of 6 individual plates. Garnish each with a fig leaf. Serve immediately.

RUSTIC BRANDADE GRATIN

Serves 4 to 8   Salt cod is a kind of dried fish that has long been a staple in the Mediterranean countries and is becoming more and more popular in the United States and elsewhere. It can be found in Italian markets and other specialty stores. Salt cod must be soaked for two to three days to rehydrate it and remove the salt before cooking. To make the classic brandade de Morue, it is pounded with olive oil and milk into a smooth paste. There is some controversy over whether or not garlic should be added; purists prefer a simple preparation without any additional flavorings. In this version, the cod is mashed so that some of the texture remains and combined with a soft purée of potatoes and cream. This gratin can be assembled up to 12 hours ahead; refrigerate, then let return to room temperature before baking.

1¹/₂ pounds boneless salt cod

2 russet potatoes (about 1 pound), peeled

1 yellow onion, coarsely chopped

2 bay leaves

8 black peppercorns

1 cup extra-virgin olive oil

1 cup heavy cream

3 or 4 cloves garlic, minced

Kosher salt and freshly ground black pepper

1 or 2 pinches of cayenne pepper

PLACE THE COD IN A LARGE BOWL; add enough cold water to cover the fish by several inches. Soak the cod for 48 hours, in the refrigerator, changing the water twice daily.

IN A LARGE POT OVER HIGH HEAT, cook the potatoes in lightly salted boiling water until tender when pierced with a knife, about 25 minutes. Drain thoroughly and mash with a potato masher until smooth. Set aside.

IN A LARGE SAUCEPAN, COMBINE THE SOAKED COD, onion, bay leaves, and peppercorns with just enough water to cover the fish. Bring to a boil over medium-high heat, then lower the heat and simmer, covered, for 15 minutes. Remove from the heat; let the cod cool in the cooking liquid. Using a slotted spoon, remove the cod from the cooking liquid and, using your hands, flake it, removing any bones and skin. Set aside.

PREHEAT THE OVEN TO 425°F. Generously butter a 10-inch (1-quart) oval gratin dish.

Topping

3 tablespoons extra-virgin olive oil

1 cup fresh bread crumbs

Kosher salt and freshly ground black pepper

Chopped fresh flat-leaf parsley, for garnish

Thin slices of baguette, toasted, for garnish

IN A LARGE SAUCEPAN, COMBINE THE OLIVE OIL, cream, and garlic and bring to a boil over medium heat. Add the fish, lower the heat, and simmer gently for 10 minutes. Using a potato masher, gently mash the fish into the cream mixture. Take care not to overmash the mixture—you want some of the flaky texture to remain. Gently fold in the mashed potatoes. Season to taste with salt, black pepper, and cayenne. Transfer the mixture to the prepared gratin dish.

TO MAKE THE TOPPING: In a small sauté pan, heat the olive oil over medium-high heat. Add the bread crumbs and toss until they have absorbed all the oil. Continue cooking, stirring constantly, until lightly browned and crispy. Remove from the heat and season to taste with salt and pepper.

SPRINKLE THE TOASTED BREAD CRUMBS evenly over the top of the gratin. Place the gratin dish on a sturdy baking sheet. Bake until bubbly, golden, and browning on the edges, about 30 minutes. Let rest for 5 minutes before serving. Garnish with the parsley and spread on the baguette toasts.

HAM, CHEESE, *and* ASPARAGUS GRATIN

Serves 6 When asparagus firsts shows up in the spring it's great simply blanched or steamed—those delicate spears need nothing more than a brush of melted butter or a lemony vinaigrette. But when the heartier late-season asparagus shows up, it's good to use it in more complex preparations. The flavor and texture of asparagus are nicely complemented by the sweet-salty bite of Westphalian ham and the nutty richness of Gruyère. Paper-thin slices of prosciutto or domestic ham will also work well here, but for the cheese, stick with the imported stuff; there's just no substitute for Gruyère.

12 to 18 thick asparagus spears, trimmed and peeled

6 to 12 thin slices (about 4 ounces) Westphalian or other good-quality ham

$^1/_2$ cup freshly grated Gruyère

Freshly ground black pepper

PREHEAT THE BROILER. Generously butter an 8 by 10-inch ($1^1/_2$-quart) gratin dish.

BRING A LARGE, WIDE SAUTÉ PAN OF WATER TO A BOIL over high heat. Add the asparagus and cook until just tender, 2 to 3 minutes. Remove with a slotted spoon or tongs and plunge into ice water to stop the cooking. Drain well and pat dry.

WRAP 2 OR 3 ASPARAGUS SPEARS together in each slice or two of ham. Place the bundles in a single layer in the prepared gratin dish. Sprinkle the Gruyère and a few grindings of pepper evenly over the tops.

PLACE THE GRATIN DISH ON A STURDY BAKING SHEET. Set under the broiler, about 4 inches from the heat source, and broil until the cheese is melted and golden, 3 to 5 minutes. Serve immediately.

GRATINÉED LEMON-GARLIC SHRIMP

Serves 4 to 6   This light and elegant dish can be assembled, baked, and served in all of half an hour. Keep a bag or two of frozen peeled shrimp on hand in the freezer and you'll always be luxuriously prepared for unexpected company. Use a metal gratin dish or ovenproof skillet to make this a one-dish meal.

4 tablespoons extra-virgin olive oil

3 tablespoons minced fresh flat-leaf parsley

3 tablespoons freshly squeezed lemon juice

1 tablespoon freshly grated lemon zest

2 tablespoons capers, drained and chopped

2 cloves garlic, minced

1 pound (about 24) large shrimp, peeled, deveined, and patted dry

$^1/_2$ cup fresh bread crumbs

PREHEAT THE BROILER. In a large bowl, combine 3 tablespoons of the olive oil, the parsley, lemon juice and zest, capers, and garlic; mix well.

HEAT THE REMAINING 1 TABLESPOON OLIVE OIL in a 12-inch ($1^1/_2$-quart) oval stainless steel, copper, or cast-iron gratin dish over medium-high heat.

ADD THE SHRIMP TO THE BOWL with the parsley mixture; pat the mixture onto the shrimp so that all sides are lightly coated, letting the extra fall back into the bowl. Transfer the shrimp to the hot gratin dish and cook until just beginning to turn pink, about 4 minutes.

MEANWHILE, ADD THE BREAD CRUMBS to the remaining parsley mixture and toss to mix. When the shrimp are sizzling, sprinkle the bread-crumb mixture over the top.

PLACE THE GRATIN DISH ON A STURDY BAKING SHEET. Set under the broiler, about 4 inches from the heat source, and broil until the crumbs are golden and crispy and the shrimp are cooked through, 4 to 5 minutes. Serve immediately.

GRATINÉED OYSTERS *and* CLAMS

Serves 4 to 6   Some people won't eat raw oysters and clams, but will happily tuck into these crispy-topped broiled morsels. Always buy live shellfish from a reputable fishmonger with a high turnover, and keep them refrigerated in an open or lightly covered container so that they can breathe. Only use oysters and clams that are tightly closed—the harder they are to open, the fresher they are. Discard any that fail to close to the touch. Oysters and clams are at their best in the fall and winter months.

18 fresh live oysters, in their shells

18 fresh live clams, in their shells

Rock salt, for baking

Topping

2 cups fresh bread crumbs

¹/₂ cup minced fresh flat-leaf parsley

3 tablespoons freshly squeezed lemon juice

1 tablespoon freshly grated lemon zest

6 tablespoons unsalted butter, melted

Kosher salt and freshly ground black pepper

TO OPEN THE SHELLFISH, wrap an oyster or clam in a kitchen towel so that the hinge end is showing. Using an oyster knife, insert the blade into the seam near the hinge and twist to open. Slide the knife along the inside of the top shell to release the abductor muscle and remove the top shell. Repeat with the remaining oysters and clams.

PREHEAT THE BROILER. Spread rock salt to a depth of about ¹/₂ inch in a baking sheet. Nestle the oysters and clams in their half shells gently into the salt so that they are stable.

TO MAKE THE TOPPING: In a medium bowl, combine the bread crumbs, parsley, and lemon juice and zest. Drizzle the melted butter over the bread-crumb mixture and toss until the bread crumbs have absorbed all of the butter. Season to taste with salt and pepper.

SPRINKLE THE TOPPING evenly over the oysters and clams. Set under the broiler, about 4 inches from the heat source, and broil until heated through and the bread crumbs are golden and crispy, about 5 minutes. Serve immediately.

ARTICHOKE CROWNS
STUFFED *with* SAFFRON-SCENTED CRAB

Serves 6 These artichokes topped with creamy, golden, saffron-scented crabmeat make an elegant special-occasion starter. Choose large artichokes, because you'll be trimming away all of the leaves and choke and using only the meaty base, or "crown." Saffron is the world's most expensive spice because it takes more than 4,300 crocus blossoms to produce enough (hand-picked!) stigmas to make a single ounce. It's worth the expense, though; it only takes a pinch to add a beautiful golden hue and subtle but distinctive flavor to foods.

6 large artichokes, trimmed
(see Note on page 24)

Topping

1 cup fresh bread crumbs

3 tablespoons unsalted butter, melted

Kosher salt and freshly ground black pepper

1 tablespoon unsalted butter

1 1/2 tablespoons all-purpose flour

1/2 cup heavy cream

1/3 cup clam juice

Pinch of saffron

Kosher salt and freshly ground black pepper

1/2 pound fresh lump crabmeat, picked over to remove any cartilage or shell bits

BRING A LARGE POT OF SALTED WATER TO A BOIL over high heat. Add the artichokes and cook until a thin-bladed knife can be easily inserted into the bottom of the arti-choke, 15 to 25 minutes. Drain and place the artichokes upside down on a clean kitchen towel; let cool.

PREHEAT THE BROILER. Lightly butter a 9 by 13-inch (3-quart) gratin dish.

TO MAKE THE TOPPING: In a small bowl, combine the bread crumbs and butter; toss until the bread crumbs have absorbed all of the butter. Season to taste with salt and pepper and set aside.

CAREFULLY REMOVE THE REMAINING LEAVES from the cooled artichokes. Using a melon baller or small, sharp-edged spoon, scrape away the fuzzy chokes. With a sharp knife, trim the outside of the artichoke crowns to a smooth shape. Transfer the crowns to the prepared gratin dish and set aside.

continued

IN A MEDIUM SAUCEPAN, MELT THE BUTTER over medium-high heat. Add the flour and cook, whisking constantly, for 1 minute. Whisk in the cream, clam juice, and saffron. Whisking constantly, bring to a boil and cook until thickened, about 2 minutes. Season to taste with salt and pepper. Remove from the heat and add the crab; mix gently with a fork so that the crab is coated with sauce but remains in small chunks.

SPOON THE CRAB MIXTURE INTO THE ARTICHOKE crowns, dividing it evenly. Sprinkle the topping over the crab. Place the gratin dish on a sturdy baking sheet. Set under the broiler, about 4 inches from the heat source, and broil until deep, golden brown, 2 to 3 minutes. Serve immediately.

NOTE: To trim artichokes, working with one artichoke at a time, cut off the stalk flush with the base of the artichoke, then remove the outermost leaves to reveal the sides of the pale, cream-colored heart. Cut off the top about an inch above the base. As each artichoke is trimmed, rub the cut surfaces with lemon to prevent discoloring, or drop them into a bowl of cold water with the juice of 1 lemon.

Artichokes, a kind of thistle, have been around since ancient times. Today, most of the artichokes we find at the market are cultivated in Castroville, the self-proclaimed "artichoke capital of the world," near California's Monterey coast. Don't think of artichokes merely as leaves to be dipped in lemon butter; their tender bases can be topped with all kinds of wonderful fillings, an experience well worth the effort it takes to clean and prepare the crowns

GRATINÉED KALE *and* BACON SOUP

Serves 4 to 6   Quick, easy, and healthy, this hearty soup is a great standby for any cook's repertoire. It goes together in about 30 minutes, although the flavors here are especially good with homemade chicken stock, if you have time. Kale, a superpower among the nutritious dark leafy greens, is loaded with fiber and vitamins.

1 tablespoon olive oil

4 thick slices bacon, cut into
¹/₄-inch dice

1 large yellow onion, finely chopped

3 large cloves garlic, minced

1 tablespoon minced fresh sage

¹/₄ teaspoon red pepper flakes

1 teaspoon freshly grated lemon
zest (optional)

Kosher salt and freshly ground
black pepper

1 bunch (about 1 pound) fresh kale,
sliced into ¹/₂-inch ribbons

5 to 6 cups chicken stock (page 10)
or canned low-sodium broth

1 (15-ounce) can navy or other small
white beans, rinsed and drained

Topping

4 to 6 slices fresh bread, cut into
¹/₂-inch cubes (about 2 to 3 cups),
toasted

¹/₂ cup freshly grated Parmesan

1 cup freshly grated Gruyère or
Emmenthaler

IN A LARGE SAUCEPAN OR SOUP POT, heat the olive oil over medium heat. Add the bacon and cook until golden and beginning to crisp. Add the onion and cook, stirring occasionally, until translucent, 2 to 3 minutes. Add the garlic and cook, stirring constantly, until the mixture begins to caramelize, about 5 minutes. Add the sage, red pepper flakes, and lemon zest. Season to taste with salt and black pepper. Add the kale and stir to coat the leaves with oil. Add the chicken stock and beans and bring to a boil. Cook, stirring occasionally, until the kale is tender and all the flavors have melded, about 10 minutes. (Do not overcook, as the kale should retain its fresh flavor.)

PREHEAT THE BROILER. Divide the hot soup evenly among 4 to 6 ovenproof soup bowls. In a small bowl, combine the cheeses and toss well. Arrange the croutons over the bowls to cover the soup as completely as possible and sprinkle the cheeses evenly over the croutons. Place the soup dishes on a sturdy baking sheet. Set under the broiler, about 4 inches from the heat source, and broil until the cheese is golden and beginning to brown, about 3 to 5 minutes. Serve immediately.

TRADITIONAL fRENCH ONION SOUP

Serves 4 to 6   The celebrated gratinéed soup of France, with Gruyère cheese melted over slices of French bread floating in a bubbling-hot, rich beef broth thickly laced with onions, makes a warm and comforting lunch or supper dish on a cold day. You can make the soup ahead of time; just return it to a boil in the pot before ladling it into deep soup bowls and topping it with the bread and cheese. Serve with a crisp green salad. Herbes de Provence is a fragrant and flavorful blend of dried herbs, usually including basil, oregano, thyme, and lavender. It's available in specialty foods stores or well-stocked supermarkets.

3 tablespoons unsalted butter or olive oil

5 large yellow onions, cut into $^{1}/_{4}$-inch slices

1 tablespoon all-purpose flour

$^{1}/_{2}$ teaspoon herbes de Provence

1 cup dry white wine

5 cups beef stock or 1 (10-ounce) can beef consommé diluted with 3 cups water

$^{1}/_{2}$ sweet baguette, cut into $^{1}/_{2}$-inch slices, toasted

2 to 3 cups freshly grated Gruyère

IN A LARGE SOUP POT, melt the butter over high heat. Add the onions, reduce the heat to medium, and cook, stirring often, until the onions are caramelized and very tender, about 40 minutes. Stir in the flour and herbes de Provence. Raise the heat to high and add the wine; cook for 2 minutes. Add the beef stock and bring to a boil. Lower the heat to medium and cook until the flavors have melded, about 30 minutes.

PREHEAT THE OVEN TO 400°F. Divide the soup evenly among 4 to 6 ovenproof soup bowls. Arrange the toasted baguette slices over the surface of each soup, covering the soup completely. Mound the Gruyère evenly over the tops of the baguette slices.

PLACE THE SOUP DISHES ON A STURDY BAKING SHEET. Bake until bubbly, golden, and browning on the edges, 10 to 15 minutes. Serve immediately (and warn diners that the soup is very hot!).

BLACK BEAN SOUP

Serves 6 to 8 This black bean soup, finished with a thick topping of cheese and garnished with fresh cilantro, is spicy and comforting. You can stir in extra fresh cilantro leaves at the end for a stronger herbal note, or add more chipotle chiles for a spicier soup. It also freezes well.

1 cup dried black beans, rinsed, soaked for 4 hours, and drained

2 tablespoons olive oil

2 large red onions, finely diced

4 celery stalks, finely diced

4 cloves garlic, minced

2 tablespoons ground cumin

1 (28-ounce) can crushed tomatoes

1 or 2 canned chipotle chiles in adobo sauce

1 tablespoon adobo sauce

$^1/_4$ cup chopped fresh cilantro

2 bay leaves

16 ounces frozen corn

Topping

1$^1/_2$ cups crushed tortilla chips

1$^1/_2$ cups freshly grated Cheddar

1$^1/_2$ cups freshly grated Monterey Jack

Fresh cilantro leaves, for garnish

IN A LARGE SOUP POT, combine the soaked beans with enough fresh cold water to cover the beans by about 2 inches. Bring to a boil, then lower the heat and simmer until just tender, 50 to 60 minutes.

IN A LARGE SAUTÉ PAN, HEAT THE OLIVE OIL over medium-high heat. Reserve $^1/_4$ cup of the onion and $^1/_4$ cup of the celery in a bowl; add the remaining onion and celery to the pan and cook, stirring occasionally, until the onions are translucent and the celery is tender. Add the garlic and cumin and cook, stirring occasionally, for 3 minutes.

ADD THE ONION MIXTURE, the tomatoes, chipotle chile(s), adobo sauce, chopped cilantro, and bay leaves to the bean pot and stir to combine. Bring to a boil, then reduce the heat and simmer until the beans are very tender and the flavors have melded, about 1 hour. (If the soup gets too thick, you may need to add some water.) Stir in the corn and simmer for 5 minutes. Discard the bay leaves.

PREHEAT THE BROILER. To make the topping, combine tortilla crumbs, cheeses, with reserved onion and celery and toss to mix. Divide the hot soup evenly among 6 or 8 oven-proof soup bowls and mound the tortilla-crumb mixture evenly over the tops. Place the soup bowls on a sturdy baking sheet. Set under the broiler, about 4 inches from the heat source, and broil until golden and bubbly, 3 to 5 minutes. Garnish with the cilantro leaves and serve immediately.

SUMPTUOUS SIDES

Zucchini Custard Gratin

Fennel, Onion, and Orange Gratin

Gratinéed Spinach with Pine Nuts
and Golden Raisins

Butternut Squash and Pecan Gratin
with Goat Cheese

Lemony Artichoke and Onion Gratin

Corn, Tomato, and Basil Gratin

Crispy Herbed Tomato Gratin

Gratinéed Eggplant in Tomato Sauce

Ratatouille Gratin

Anchovy-Scented Red Bell Pepper
and Tomato Gratin

Tomato and Chèvre Gratin

Minted English Pea Gratin

Gratinéed Shallots à la Crème

Creamy Leek Gratin

ZUCCHINI CUSTARD GRATIN

Serves 4 to 6   In this elegant dish, a creamy, savory custard harbors thin slices of lightly cooked, garlic-scented zucchini. You can assemble it in individual ramekins for a picturesque first course, or make it in a gratin dish and serve it family style alongside your favorite roast meat. It pairs especially well with leg of lamb. Use young, slender, firm zucchini because, as they mature, zucchini develop more seeds and become watery.

2 tablespoons unsalted butter

1 clove garlic, minced

1^1/$_2$ pounds zucchini, trimmed and cut into ^{1}/$_4$-inch slices

^{1}/$_2$ teaspoon minced fresh thyme

3 eggs

1 cup heavy cream

^{1}/$_4$ teaspoon freshly ground nutmeg

Kosher salt and freshly ground black pepper

^{1}/$_2$ cup freshly grated Gruyère or Emmenthaler

PREHEAT THE OVEN TO 350°F. Generously butter an 8 by 10-inch (1^1/$_2$-quart) gratin dish.

IN A LARGE SAUTÉ PAN, melt the butter over medium-high heat. Add the garlic and cook until fragrant, about 1 minute. Add the zucchini and thyme and cook until the liquid is released, about 2 minutes. Using a slotted spoon, transfer the zucchini mixture to the prepared gratin dish. Discard the remaining liquid.

IN A MEDIUM BOWL, whisk together the eggs, cream, and nutmeg, and season with salt and pepper. Pour the custard mixture evenly over the zucchini and sprinkle the cheese over the top. Place the gratin on a sturdy baking sheet. Bake until the custard is set but still jiggly in the middle, about 30 minutes. Serve immediately.

FENNEL, ONION, *and* ORANGE GRATIN

Serves 4 to 6   Mild, licorice-flavored fennel is combined with sweet onions and orange zest in this light, crispy-topped gratin. Choose firm bulbs of fennel with their bright green, feathery fronds still attached. After trimming, you can use the tops for garnish or add them to salads. Fennel is a natural accompaniment to grilled fish.

2 large yellow onions, cut into ¹/₂-inch wedges

2 large fennel bulbs (about 2 pounds), stems, feathery tops, and any bruised outer stalks trimmed, cut into ¹/₂-inch slices

2 tablespoons olive oil

1 teaspoon freshly grated orange zest

Kosher salt and freshly ground black pepper

Topping

¹/₂ cup fresh bread crumbs

¹/₂ cup freshly grated mozzarella

¹/₄ cup freshly grated Parmesan

2 tablespoons extra-virgin olive oil

Kosher salt and freshly ground black pepper

PREHEAT THE OVEN TO 350°F. Generously butter a 9-inch (1-quart) square gratin dish.

IN A LARGE BOWL, COMBINE THE ONIONS, fennel, olive oil, orange zest, and salt and pepper to taste; toss until the onion and fennel are coated with the oil. Transfer the onion mixture to the prepared gratin dish. Place the gratin on a sturdy baking sheet. Bake until the onions and fennel are tender, about 30 minutes.

TO MAKE THE TOPPING: In a small bowl, combine the bread crumbs and cheeses and toss to mix. Drizzle the olive oil over the bread-crumb mixture and toss until the bread crumbs have absorbed all of the oil. Season to taste with salt and pepper. Set aside.

REMOVE THE GRATIN FROM THE OVEN and sprinkle the topping evenly over the fennel mixture. Return to the oven and continue baking until the cheese is melted and the top is golden and crispy, about 20 minutes. Serve immediately.

GRATINÉED SPINACH *with* PINE NUTS *and* GOLDEN RAISINS

Serves 4 to 6 Popeye never had spinach like this: tender and creamy, flavored with nutmeg and sweet raisins, all tucked under a golden crust. If you're in a hurry, use bags of prewashed spinach and trim off the long stems. Two pounds of spinach may look like a lot at first, but it cooks down to about 2 cups very quickly. Use tongs to turn the spinach while it cooks so that all the leaves are exposed to the heat and wilt evenly. The tenderizing effect of soaking raisins is worth the extra step.

4 tablespoons unsalted butter

2 pounds spinach, stemmed, rinsed, and well dried

1 small yellow onion, finely chopped

1 clove garlic, minced

2 tablespoons all-purpose flour

1 cup chicken stock (page 10) or canned low-sodium broth

$^1/_2$ cup heavy cream

$^1/_4$ teaspoon red pepper flakes

$^1/_8$ teaspoon freshly grated nutmeg

1 cup freshly grated pecorino Romano

$^1/_4$ cup pine nuts, toasted (see Note page 33)

$^1/_4$ cup golden raisins, plumped in hot water to cover for 30 minutes, then drained

Kosher salt and freshly ground black pepper

PREHEAT THE OVEN TO 375°F. Generously butter a 7 by 9-inch (1-quart) gratin dish.

IN A LARGE SAUTÉ PAN, melt 2 tablespoons of the butter over high heat. Add the spinach and cook, turning with tongs, until completely wilted and very tender. Transfer the spinach to a fine-mesh strainer. Press on the spinach to remove any liquid—the back of a wooden spoon or ladle works well for this. Chop coarsely and set aside.

IN A SMALL SAUCEPAN, melt the remaining 2 tablespoons butter over medium heat. Add the onion and cook until just beginning to caramelize, about 4 minutes. Add the garlic and cook for 1 minute. Add the flour and cook, stirring constantly, until just beginning to take on a straw color. Add the chicken stock and bring to a boil. Cook, whisking constantly, until the sauce thickens, about 2 minutes. Whisk in the cream, red pepper flakes, and nutmeg.

REMOVE THE PAN FROM THE HEAT and stir in the cheese, pine nuts, and raisins. Fold in the spinach. Season to taste with salt and pepper. Transfer to the prepared gratin dish.

Topping

$^1/_2$ cup fresh bread crumbs

$^1/_2$ cup freshly grated pecorino
Romano

2 tablespoons unsalted butter,
melted

Kosher salt and freshly ground
black pepper

TO MAKE THE TOPPING: In a bowl, combine the bread crumbs and cheese; drizzle with the melted butter and toss until the bread crumbs have absorbed all of the butter. Season to taste with salt and pepper.

SPRINKLE THE TOPPING OVER THE THE SPINACH. Place the gratin on a sturdy baking sheet. Bake until golden and bubbly, about 30 minutes. Let rest for 5 minutes before serving.

NOTE: To toast nuts, preheat oven to 350°F. Spread the nuts on a baking sheet or in a shallow pan. Bake, stirring once or twice, until lightly browned and fragrant, 5 to 10 minutes. Let cool. Or, place in a small, dry skillet over medium heat. Toast, stirring often, until golden; watch carefully to prevent burning. Transfer to a plate to cool when just a shade lighter than desired; the nuts will continue to toast as they cool.

BUTTERNUT SQUASH *and* PECAN GRATIN *with* GOAT CHEESE

Serves 6 to 8 These pretty slices of squash are accented with the tangy bite of goat cheese and the rich crunch of pecans—a combination so good, you can serve this dish at Thanksgiving instead of sweet potatoes. Paired with a substantial salad, it can be a satisfying meatless main course; or serve it with thin slices of roasted meat or chicken.

2 tablespoons unsalted butter

1 yellow onion, finely chopped

2 cloves garlic, minced

2 cups heavy cream

2 teaspoons kosher salt

$^1/_2$ teaspoon freshly ground black pepper

$2^1/_2$ pounds butternut squash, peeled, seeded, and cut into $^1/_4$-inch slices

$1^1/_2$ cups pecans, toasted and coarsely chopped

4 ounces fresh goat cheese, crumbled

3 tablespoons chopped fresh flat-leaf parsley, for garnish

PREHEAT THE OVEN TO 350°F. Generously butter a 9 by 13-inch (3-quart) gratin dish.

IN A LARGE SAUTÉ PAN, MELT THE BUTTER over medium-high heat. Add the onion and cook until lightly browned, about 5 minutes. Add the garlic and cook for 1 minute. Add the cream, salt, and pepper and bring to a boil. Add the squash and half of the pecans and return to a boil. Lower the heat and simmer gently for 5 minutes.

TRANSFER HALF OF THE SQUASH MIXTURE to the prepared gratin dish. Dot with half of the goat cheese. Cover with the remaining squash mixture and sprinkle the remaining goat cheese over the top.

PLACE THE GRATIN ON A STURDY BAKING SHEET. Bake until the squash is very tender, the cream is mostly absorbed, and the top is golden, about 45 minutes. Remove from the oven and sprinkle with the remaining pecans and the parsley. Let rest for 10 minutes before serving.

LEMONY ARTICHOKE *and* ONION GRATIN

Serves 4 to 6 Because this gratin uses frozen artichokes, it can be enjoyed year-round, although if fresh are available, by all means go ahead and use them. (Trim them to the heart and boil or steam until tender before you begin.) Serve this in individual dishes as a first course or as a flavorful side with grilled fish or steak. Artichokes are notoriously difficult to pair with wine, but in this dish they are tamed by the combination of sweet onions and cheese in a way that invites a glass of dry Madeira, or even a Cabernet Franc.

2 tablespoons olive oil

1 large yellow onion, peeled and cut into $^{1}/_{4}$-inch slices

16 ounces frozen artichoke hearts, thawed, or 2 (15-ounce) cans artichoke hearts, rinsed and drained

1 large clove garlic, minced

1 teaspoon freshly grated lemon zest

1 cup dry white wine, vegetable stock (page 11), or canned vegetable broth

3 tablespoons minced fresh flat-leaf parsley

1 teaspoon herbes de Provence

Kosher salt and freshly ground black pepper

Topping

$^{1}/_{2}$ cup fresh bread crumbs

$^{1}/_{2}$ cup freshly grated mozzarella

$^{1}/_{4}$ cup freshly grated Parmesan

2 tablespoons extra-virgin olive oil

Freshly ground black pepper

PREHEAT THE OVEN TO 350°F. Generously butter a 9-inch (1-quart) square gratin dish.

IN A LARGE SAUTÉ PAN, HEAT THE OLIVE OIL over medium heat. Add the onion and cook, stirring occasionally, until golden and beginning to caramelize, about 5 minutes. Add the artichokes, garlic, and lemon zest and cook for 1 minute. Add the wine, parsley, and herbes de Provence and bring to a boil. Cook until reduced by half, about 10 minutes. Season to taste with salt and pepper.

TO MAKE THE TOPPING: In a small bowl, combine the bread crumbs and cheeses. Drizzle the olive oil over the bread-crumb mixture and toss until the bread crumbs have absorbed all of the oil. Season to taste with pepper and set aside.

TRANSFER THE ARTICHOKE MIXTURE to the prepared gratin dish. Sprinkle the topping evenly over. Place the gratin on a sturdy baking sheet. Bake until the cheese is melted and the top is golden and crispy, 20 to 30 minutes. Serve immediately.

CORN, TOMATO, *and* BASIL GRATIN

Serves 6 This is a great dish for showcasing the sweet, fresh corn of high summer. White corn has become more and more readily available at the markets, but as it is very sweet, you may prefer the traditional flavor of yellow corn here. Sugar in corn kernels converts to starch soon after picking, so make sure that you buy fresh corn that hasn't been sitting at the stand too long.

3 cups fresh corn kernels (about 5 ears), or 16 ounces frozen corn, thawed

1¹/₂ pounds ripe plum (Roma) tomatoes, coarsely chopped

³/₄ cup loosely packed fresh basil leaves, plus extra for garnish, all cut into chiffonade

1 cup heavy cream

1 teaspoon kosher salt

Topping

1 cup fresh bread crumbs

3 tablespoons unsalted butter, melted

Freshly ground black pepper

PREHEAT THE OVEN TO 350°F. Generously butter a 12-inch (1¹/₂-quart) oval gratin dish.

IN A LARGE BOWL, COMBINE THE CORN, tomatoes, the ³/₄ cup basil chiffonade, the cream, and salt and toss to mix. Transfer the corn mixture to the prepared gratin dish. Place the gratin dish on a sturdy baking sheet. Bake for 30 minutes.

MEANWHILE, MAKE THE TOPPING: In a small bowl, combine the bread crumbs and butter; toss until the bread crumbs have absorbed all of the butter. Season to taste with a generous amount of pepper.

REMOVE THE GRATIN FROM THE OVEN and sprinkle the topping evenly over the corn mixture. Return to the oven and continue baking until bubbly, golden, and crispy, about 30 minutes. Let rest for 5 minutes before serving. Garnish with basil chiffonade.

NOTE: To cut corn kernels from the cob, break or cut the cobs in half. Hold a cob half upright, flat end down, and use a sharp knife to cut straight down between the kernels and the cob, avoiding the fibrous material at the base of the kernels and surface of the cob.

CRISPY HERBED TOMATO GRATIN

Serves 4 to 6 This simply made topping of fragrant oregano, parsley, garlic, and bread crumbs combines with the sweet juices of just-picked, sun-ripened tomatoes to make a warm, herb-scented side dish. Chop the herbs immediately before using or they will discolor and lose some of their fresh intensity.

4 to 6 ripe tomatoes, halved horizontally

Topping

1 cup fresh bread crumbs

$^1/_4$ cup minced fresh flat-leaf parsley

3 large cloves garlic, minced

1 tablespoon minced fresh oregano

$^1/_2$ teaspoon kosher salt

Freshly ground black pepper

3 tablespoons extra-virgin olive oil

PREHEAT THE OVEN TO 375°F. Arrange the tomato halves, cut sides up, $^1/_2$ inch apart in an 8 by 11-inch (2-quart) gratin dish.

TO MAKE THE TOPPING: In a small bowl, combine the bread crumbs, parsley, garlic, oregano, and salt and toss to mix. Season with pepper to taste. Drizzle the olive oil over the bread-crumb mixture and toss until the bread crumbs have absorbed all of the oil. Divide the topping evenly among the tomatoes, mounding it on top.

PLACE THE GRATIN ON A STURDY BAKING SHEET. Bake until the topping is golden and crispy and the tomatoes are cooked through but still hold their shape, about 20 minutes. Serve immediately.

GRATINÉED EGGPLANT *in* TOMATO SAUCE

Serves 4 to 6 Freshness and seasonality are critical when just a few ingredients are combined in a simple dish. Select an unblemished, deep purple eggplant; plump, vine-ripened tomatoes; and a firm, fresh-smelling bell pepper for this variation on the classic eggplant Parmesan. This recipe can easily be doubled to serve as a main dish for lunch or supper.

1 large eggplant (about 1 pound), sliced into ¹/₂-inch rounds

2 tablespoons olive oil

1 yellow onion, chopped

2 large cloves garlic, minced

1 red bell pepper, cored, seeded, and cut into ¹/₂-inch dice

1 pound ripe tomatoes, peeled, seeded, and cut into ¹/₂-inch dice

¹/₂ cup water

¹/₂ cup freshly grated Parmesan or pecorino Romano

¹/₂ cup freshly grated Gruyère or Emmenthaler

PREHEAT THE OVEN TO 350°F. Generously grease an 8 by 10-inch (1¹/₂-quart) gratin dish with olive oil. Generously grease a large baking sheet with olive oil.

ARRANGE THE EGGPLANT in a single layer on the prepared baking sheet. Turn the slices over once so that both sides are lightly coated with oil. Bake until tender, 20 to 30 minutes.

MEANWHILE, IN A LARGE SAUTÉ PAN, heat the olive oil over medium heat. Add the onion and cook, stirring occasionally, until it begins to caramelize, about 5 minutes. Add the garlic and cook for 1 minute. Add the bell pepper and cook for 1 minute. Add the tomatoes and water and cook until the tomatoes begin to break down and thicken. Remove from the heat.

SPREAD ¹/₂ CUP OF THE TOMATO SAUCE over the bottom of the prepared gratin dish. Arrange half of the eggplant slices over the sauce. Spoon half of the remaining sauce over the eggplant and sprinkle 2 tablespoons of the Parmesan over the sauce. Repeat with remaining eggplant and sauce. Sprinkle the remaining Parmesan and the Gruyère evenly over the top.

PLACE THE GRATIN ON A STURDY BAKING SHEET. Bake until the cheese is melted and the top is golden and bubbly, about 30 minutes. Let rest for 5 minutes before serving.

RATATOUILLE GRATIN

Serves 8 to 10 This gratin features all the elements of the well-loved tomato-and-eggplant dish ratatouille, melded together under a crunchy-cheesy topping. Eat this gratin piping hot, right from the oven, but save some leftovers—like its namesake, it's often even better reheated or at room temperature the next day.

2 pounds ripe plum (Roma) tomatoes

1 large eggplant (about 1¼ pounds), cut into 1-inch dice

3 tablespoons olive oil

3 yellow onions, thinly sliced

3 red bell peppers, cored, seeded, and thinly sliced

4 cloves garlic, thinly sliced

½ teaspoon herbes de Provence

½ teaspoon red pepper flakes

2 cups firmly packed fresh basil leaves, plus ¼ cup, cut into chiffonade, for garnish

3 small zucchini (about ¾ pound), trimmed and thinly sliced

PREHEAT THE OVEN TO 350°F. Generously grease a baking sheet or dish with olive oil.

THINLY SLICE HALF OF THE TOMATOES and set aside. Coarsely chop the remaining tomatoes and set aside.

ARRANGE THE EGGPLANT in the prepared dish and drizzle with 1 tablespoon of the olive oil; toss to coat. Bake until the eggplant has softened and is just beginning to take on color, about 30 minutes.

MEANWHILE, IN A LARGE SAUTÉ PAN, heat the remaining 2 tablespoons olive oil over high heat. Add the onions and cook, stirring often, until translucent, about 5 minutes. Add the bell peppers, garlic, herbes de Provence, and red pepper flakes and cook until the bell peppers are softened, about 5 minutes. Add the chopped tomatoes and cook until they have softened and the juices are beginning to evaporate. Remove from the heat.

GENEROUSLY GREASE a 9 by 13-inch (3-quart) gratin dish with olive oil. Leave the oven temperature at 350°F.

IN A BOWL, TOSS THE ROASTED EGGPLANT with half of the whole basil leaves. Arrange half of the eggplant mixture in the prepared gratin dish and scatter one-third of the remaining whole basil leaves over the eggplant. Cover with half of the tomato mixture. Scatter another one-third of

continued

Topping

$^1/_2$ cup fresh bread crumbs

$^1/_4$ cup freshly grated Parmesan

1 tablespoon olive oil

the basil leaves over the tomato mixture, followed by the remaining eggplant, the remaining tomato mixture, and the last of the basil leaves. Carefully arrange the zucchini and tomato slices in alternating rows over the eggplant, overlapping the slices slightly within their rows and overlapping the rows slightly in order to completely cover the gratin in a decorative pattern.

TO MAKE THE TOPPING: In a small bowl, combine the bread crumbs and Parmesan. Drizzle the olive oil over the bread-crumb mixture and toss until the bread crumbs have absorbed all of the oil.

SPRINKLE THE TOPPING over the zucchini and tomato slices. Place the gratin on a sturdy baking sheet. Bake until the cheese is melted and the top is golden, crispy, and bubbly, 30 to 45 minutes. Let rest for 20 to 30 minutes before serving. Garnish with the basil chiffonade. Serve hot, warm, or at room temperature.

Always choose young, firm, heavy eggplants and eat within a day or so of purchase. They become bitter with age as they develop more seeds along with a grainy texture. The skin is edible when eggplants are young but the tough skins of more-mature fruits should be removed. Should you end up with a not-so-young specimen, the consistency will be improved if you cut it into $^1/_4$-inch slices, sprinkle with salt, and let drain in a colander set over a plate for about an hour. Rinse, pat dry, and use as directed in the recipe.

ANCHOVY-SCENTED RED BELL PEPPER
and TOMATO GRATIN

Serves 4 to 6 This recipe is for roasted peppers, featuring a delicious blend of tomatoes, anchovies, garlic, and olive oil. It's important here to use good-quality anchovies packed either in extra-virgin olive oil or salt—the latter must be rinsed, soaked, and filleted before using. If you're worried about the anchovies dominating this dish, don't be concerned. They add a rich, savory, earthy nuance that deepens the flavors of this robust dish. Serve alongside beef or with grilled, firm-fleshed fish.

2 pounds firm, ripe tomatoes, cut into 2-inch chunks

2 large red bell peppers, cored, seeded, and cut into 2-inch pieces

6 anchovy fillets, drained and chopped

4 cloves garlic, thinly sliced

3 tablespoons olive oil

Topping

$^1/_2$ cup fresh bread crumbs

$^1/_4$ cup freshly grated Parmesan

$^1/_4$ cup pine nuts

2 tablespoons extra-virgin olive oil

PREHEAT THE OVEN TO 350°F. In a bowl, combine the tomatoes, bell peppers, anchovies, garlic, and olive oil; toss to mix. Transfer to a 12-inch ($1^1/_2$-quart) oval gratin dish. Place on a sturdy baking sheet and bake for 45 minutes.

MEANWHILE, MAKE THE TOPPING: In a small bowl, combine the bread crumbs, Parmesan, and pine nuts. Drizzle the olive oil over the bread-crumb mixture and toss until the bread crumbs have absorbed all of the oil.

REMOVE THE GRATIN FROM THE OVEN and sprinkle the topping evenly over the tomatoes and peppers. Return to the oven and continue baking until golden and crispy, about 15 minutes. Let rest for 5 minutes before serving.

TOMATO *and* CHÈVRE GRATIN

Serves 4 to 6 Not many years ago, it was hard to find goat cheese in the supermarket; now almost any well-stocked market carries a selection. Some of the best goat cheese is produced by artisanal makers in the United States. Goat cheese comes in all shapes and ages, from the softest, creamiest types sold in tubs to hard-pressed wheels aged for years. For this recipe, choose a medium-soft log of fresh goat cheese; these slice or crumble nicely.

2 pounds ripe tomatoes, quartered

1 yellow onion, cut into ¹/₂-inch wedges

2 large cloves garlic, minced

1 teaspoon herbes de Provence

Kosher salt and freshly ground black pepper

2 tablespoons olive oil

1 roasted red bell pepper, peeled and thinly sliced (see Note)

1 cup black olives, pitted and coarsely chopped

3 tablespoons minced fresh flat-leaf parsley

10 ounces chèvre or other soft fresh goat cheese

¹/₂ cup chopped walnuts

¹/₂ cup loosely packed fresh basil leaves, cut into chiffonade, for garnish

PREHEAT THE OVEN TO 325°F. In a 12-inch (1¹/₂-quart) oval gratin dish, combine the tomatoes, onion, garlic, herbes de Provence, and salt and pepper to taste. Drizzle with the olive oil and toss to mix. Bake until the tomatoes have released their juices and the onions are very tender, 1 to 2 hours depending on the water content of the tomatoes.

REMOVE THE DISH FROM THE OVEN. Increase the oven temperature to 350°F. Sprinkle the roasted peppers, olives, and parsley over the top of the tomato mixture. Dot with the goat cheese. Return to the oven and continue baking until the goat cheese has melted, about 30 minutes. Using the back of a spoon, carefully spread the hot goat cheese more evenly over the top of the tomato mixture. Sprinkle with the walnuts. Continue baking until golden and bubbly, 15 to 20 minutes. Garnish with the basil chiffonade.

NOTE: To roast peppers, set them on a grill directly over the flame of a gas burner; alternatively, place in a preheated broiler 4 to 6 inches from the heat source. Turn as needed until the skin is blackened and charred all over. Transfer to a bowl, cover with plastic wrap, and let cool. When cool enough to handle, peel away the skins. Do not rinse.

MINTED ENGLISH PEA GRATIN

Serves 6 to 8 Eager shoppers at farmers' markets fill brown bags to overflowing with pods of plump English peas when they're in season. Although 3 pounds of the legume looks big in the bag, it yields just about a pound (3 cups) of shelled peas. It's somewhat time-consuming, but popping the pods and releasing their contents is a pleasant, relaxing task. Some people save the pods for soups, as they are tasty but require a long cooking time to become tender.

3 pounds fresh English peas, shelled (about 3 cups), or 16 ounces frozen petit peas, thawed

2 tablespoons unsalted butter

1 large yellow onion, thinly sliced

1 head Boston or butter lettuce, washed and sliced into $^1/_2$-inch ribbons

1 tablespoon all-purpose flour

1 cup heavy cream

$^1/_2$ teaspoon kosher salt

Freshly ground black pepper

$^1/_4$ cup loosely packed fresh mint leaves, plus extra for garnish, all cut into chiffonade

Topping

$1^1/_2$ cups fresh bread crumbs

4 tablespoons unsalted butter, melted

Kosher salt and freshly ground black pepper

PREHEAT THE OVEN TO 400°F. Generously butter a 12-inch ($1^1/_2$-quart) oval gratin dish.

BRING A SAUCEPAN OF WATER TO A BOIL. Add the peas and cook until they are just tender, about 5 minutes. Drain and set aside. (Omit this step if you are using frozen peas.)

IN A SAUTÉ PAN, MELT THE BUTTER over medium heat. Add the onion and cook until translucent, 2 to 3 minutes. Add the lettuce and cook, stirring until wilted. Sprikle over the flour and cook, stirring constantly, for 1 minute. Pour over the cream and bring to a boil, stirring constantly. Add the peas, salt, pepper to taste, and the $^1/_4$ cup mint leaf chiffonade and stir to combine. Transfer the mixture to the prepared gratin dish.

TO MAKE THE TOPPING: In a medium bowl, combine the bread crumbs and butter and toss until the bread crumbs have absorbed all of the butter. Season to taste with salt and pepper.

SPRINKLE THE TOPPING EVENLY OVER THE PEAS. Place the gratin on a sturdy baking sheet. Bake until golden and bubbly, about 30 minutes. Let rest for 5 minutes before serving. Garnish with mint chiffonade.

GRATINÉED SHALLOTS À LA CRÈME

Serves 4 to 6   It could be said that shallots suffer from an identity crisis. They look like small onions but are constructed like garlic, with clusters of bulbs held together at the root end. Their onion-like flavor is exceptionally mild, lending them versatility. They play the lead role in this cream-based gratin. Choose a small gratin dish, just big enough to hold the shallots so that they're touching. Though this recipe makes just a generous spoonful or two per serving, it doubles easily.

1 pound shallots, peeled (see Note)

1 cup water

2 tablespoons unsalted butter

¹/₂ teaspoon kosher salt

¹/₂ teaspoon sugar

1 cup heavy cream

1 cup crushed oiled croutons

PREHEAT THE OVEN TO 350°F. Generously butter a 6 by 8-inch (2-cup) gratin dish.

IN A SAUTÉ PAN, COMBINE THE SHALLOTS, water, butter, salt, and sugar. Bring to a boil, then lower the heat and simmer until tender and most of the liquid has evaporated, about 30 minutes. Remove from the heat, stir in the cream, and transfer the mixture to the prepared gratin dish.

PLACE THE GRATIN ON A STURDY BAKING SHEET. Bake until the shallots are very tender, about 30 minutes. Remove the gratin from the oven and sprinkle with the crushed croutons (slices of bread brushed with butter or oil, sealed in a plastic bag and smashed into crumbs with a rolling pin). Return to the oven and continue baking until golden and bubbly, about 10 minutes. Let rest for 5 minutes before serving.

NOTE: To peel shallots, cut off the root and trim the tips. Plunge them into a pot of boiling water for 1 minute. Drain. When cool enough to handle, remove the skins; they should peel easily.

CREAMY LEEK GRATIN

Serves 4 to 6 Long, slender, batonlike leeks, a mild-flavored member of the onion family, are sometimes called "poor man's asparagus." They become savory-sweet and creamy after slow cooking for this sour cream–topped gratin. Look for leeks that are about 1 1/2 inches in diameter, with dark green leaves and firm, clean stalks that are more than half white, without any dark or soft patches. If the roots are still on, all the better—stored in water, they will drink and stay fresher.

3 medium or 6 small leeks, trimmed and washed (see Note)

1 cup chicken stock (page 10) or canned low-sodium broth

2 tablespoons unsalted butter

1/4 teaspoon kosher salt

Freshly ground black pepper

Topping

1 cup sour cream

1/4 cup whole milk

Kosher salt and freshly ground black pepper

IF THE LEEKS ARE MORE THAN 2 inches in diameter, cut them in half lengthwise. Arrange the leeks in a 12-inch (1 1/2-quart) oval stainless steel or copper gratin dish. Add the stock and dot the top of the leeks with the butter. Season with the salt and pepper to taste. Cover the dish with aluminum foil and bring to a boil over medium-high heat. Lower the heat and simmer until just tender, about 10 minutes. Remove the foil and continue cooking until most of the liquid has evaporated, about 20 minutes.

PREHEAT THE BROILER. Meanwhile, make the topping: In a small bowl, whisk together the sour cream and milk. Season to taste with salt and pepper.

POUR THE SOUR CREAM MIXTURE EVENLY over the leeks. Place the gratin on a sturdy baking sheet. Set under the broiler, about 4 inches from the heat source, and broil until golden and bubbly. Let rest for 5 minutes before serving.

NOTE: To clean leeks, trim the roots from the base and any dark, tough outer leaves. Hold the white end of the leek in one hand and insert a small, sharp knife through the bulb. Make a lengthwise slit in the leek, cutting toward the green leaves. Rinse thoroughly and gently spread the leaf layers to remove any mud and grit.

PERFECT POTATOES

COUNTRY POTATO GRATIN

Serves 4 to 6 If you like the traditional combination of potatoes, garlic, and onions, but don't want to be weighed down by the equally traditional cream sauce, this is the gratin for you. Instead of cream, flavorful chicken stock is used, and the whole thing is cooked long and slow so that a good crust forms. If you like, you can sprinkle the top with grated Gruyère, Parmesan or Romano cheese.

4 large russet potatoes (about 2^1/$_2$ pounds), peeled and thinly sliced

2 yellow onions, thinly sliced

3 large cloves garlic, thinly sliced

Kosher salt and freshly ground black pepper

1^1/$_2$ cups chicken stock (page 10) or canned low-sodium broth, or more as needed

2 tablespoons unsalted butter, or more as needed

PREHEAT THE OVEN TO 350°F. Generously butter a 12-inch (1^1/$_2$-quart) oval gratin dish.

LAYER ONE-THIRD OF THE POTATO SLICES, slightly overlapping, in the prepared gratin dish. Scatter half of the onions and half of the garlic over the potatoes; season well with salt and pepper. Repeat with another one-third of the potato slices and the remaining onions and garlic. Season well with salt and pepper. End with the remaining potato slices, taking care to arrange them in an attractive pattern.

POUR THE STOCK OVER THE POTATOES; again season well with salt and pepper. Dot with the butter. Place the gratin on a sturdy baking sheet. Bake until golden and bubbly, 1 to 1^1/$_2$ hours. If the surface seems dry, dot with a little more butter or baste with a little more chicken stock halfway through cooking. Let rest for 10 minutes before serving.

SPINACH, BACON, *and* POTATO GRATIN

Serves 4 to 6 In this gratin, onions, bacon, and tender sautéed spinach are sandwiched between layers of sliced cooked potatoes to make a satisfying, savory lunch or supper dish. Top each portion with a poached egg for a hearty brunch.

6 russet potatoes (about 3 pounds), unpeeled, scrubbed

6 thick slices bacon, cut into 1/4-inch dice

1 large yellow onion, finely chopped

2 large cloves garlic, minced

Pinch of red pepper flakes

1 pound baby spinach, stemmed, rinsed, and well dried

Kosher salt and freshly ground black pepper

Freshly grated nutmeg

1/2 cup freshly grated Cheddar

1/2 cup freshly grated Parmesan

PREHEAT THE OVEN TO 400°F. Generously butter a 12-inch (1 1/2-quart) oval gratin dish.

IN A LARGE POT OVER HIGH HEAT, COOK THE POTATOES in lightly salted boiling water until tender when pierced with a knife, about 25 minutes. Drain and set aside to cool.

HEAT A LARGE SAUTÉ PAN OVER MEDIUM HEAT; add the bacon and cook until golden and the fat has been rendered, about 3 minutes. Add the onion and cook until translucent, about 2 minutes. Add the garlic and red pepper flakes and cook until fragrant, about 2 minutes. Add the spinach and cook, turning with tongs, until just beginning to wilt. Immediately remove the pan from the heat; season to taste with salt, pepper, and a few gratings of nutmeg. Transfer the spinach mixture to a fine-mesh sieve and let drain.

PEEL AND THINLY SLICE THE POTATOES. Arrange half of the slices in the prepared gratin dish. Season generously with salt and pepper. Spread the spinach mixture evenly over the top of the potatoes. Top with the remaining potato slices, taking care to arrange them in an attractive pattern. Season again with salt and pepper.

SPRINKLE THE CHEESES EVENLY OVER THE TOP. Place the gratin on a sturdy baking sheet. Bake until golden and bubbly, about 30 minutes. Let rest for 5 minutes before serving.

CELERY ROOT *and* POTATO GRATIN

Serves 6 to 8 Celery root, also known as celeriac, is a big, scruffy-looking, rootlike knob. Its skin is quite rough and must be peeled before using. The flesh underneath is creamy white with a slightly mottled look. Celery root can be eaten raw or it can be boiled alone or mixed with mashed potatoes. Cooked and puréed, it becomes smooth and creamy, with a lovely, delicate celery flavor that hints of parsley. Sliced and cooked with cream, it stars in this delicious gratin. Dry Monterey or Sonoma Jack cheese can be found in specialty food stores and is well worth the search. A low-moisture aged cheese with a concentrated flavor similar to Cheddar, it's perfect for grating.

1 cup heavy cream

1 cup whole milk

2 cloves garlic, minced

1 celery root (about 1 pound), peeled, quartered, and thinly sliced

4 Yukon gold potatoes (about 2 pounds), peeled and thinly sliced

1 teaspoon kosher salt

Freshly ground black pepper

$^1/_4$ cup freshly grated dry Monterey or Sonoma Jack

Fresh flat-leaf parsley leaves, for garnish

PREHEAT THE OVEN TO 350°F. Generously butter a 12-inch ($1^1/_2$-quart) oval gratin dish.

IN A LARGE SAUCEPAN, COMBINE THE CREAM, milk, and garlic and bring to a boil over medium heat. Add the celery root, potatoes, salt, and a few grindings of pepper and return to a boil. Lower the heat and simmer, stirring occasionally so that the slices stay separate, for about 10 minutes. Transfer the mixture to the prepared gratin dish and smooth the top. Sprinkle the cheese evenly over the top.

PLACE THE GRATIN ON A STURDY BAKING SHEET lined with aluminum foil. Bake until the potatoes are tender when pierced with the tip of a knife and the top is golden and bubbly, 50 minutes to 1 hour. Let rest for 5 minutes before serving. Garnish with the fresh parsley leaves and serve.

GREEN APPLE, YUKON GOLD, *and* SWEET POTATO GRATIN

Serves 4 to 8 Sweet potatoes combined with silky Yukon gold potatoes and tart green apples make a gratin that's especially tantalizing. Sweet potatoes are not actually related to potatoes at all—they are from the morning glory family of plants. They come in a variety of colors from yellow to bright orange. The orange ones are sometimes mistakenly called yams, although true yams are a wholly different species and not widely available in the United States. The ingredients in this gratin have similar textures but contrasting flavors to provide interest, with the sweet, starchy roots countered by the tart apples. It's excellent with roast chicken or turkey.

4 Yukon gold potatoes (about 2 pounds), peeled and thinly sliced

1 large sweet potato (about 1 pound), peeled and thinly sliced

2 cloves garlic, minced

1 large yellow onion, minced

1 tablespoon minced fresh sage

1 teaspoon minced fresh thyme

2 large green apples such as Granny Smith (about 1 pound), peeled, cored, and thinly sliced

Kosher salt and freshly ground black pepper

1 cup heavy cream

1 cup whole milk

1 tablespoon unsalted butter

1 cup freshly grated Gruyère

PREHEAT THE OVEN TO 350°F. Generously butter a 9 by 13-inch (3-quart) gratin dish.

ARRANGE ONE-QUARTER OF THE POTATO SLICES in the prepared gratin dish. Cover with half each of the sweet potato slices, garlic, onion, sage, thyme and apples. Season with salt and pepper. Repeat with another one-quarter of the potato slices and the remaining sweet potatoes, garlic, onion, sage, thyme and apples. Season again with salt and pepper. End with the remaining potatoes, taking care to arrange them in an attractive pattern.

IN A SMALL BOWL, WHISK TOGETHER THE CREAM and milk. Pour the cream mixture over the top of the potatoes. Dot with the butter and season with salt and pepper. Sprinkle the cheese over the top.

PLACE THE GRATIN ON A STURDY BAKING SHEET. Bake until the potatoes are tender when pierced with the tip of a knife and the top is golden and bubbly, about 1 hour. Let rest for 10 minutes before serving.

GRATIN DAUPHINOISE

Serves 8 to 10 Luscious heavy cream combined with the humble potato and subtle hints of garlic makes for a truly elegant dish. This rich and delectable gratin, also known as scalloped potatoes, is a perfect side with roast chicken, leg of lamb, or a standing rib roast. As the cream will often bubble up and over the edges of the dish, covering the baking sheet with aluminum foil makes for easier cleanup.

^{1}/$_4$ cup unsalted butter, at room temperature

1 clove garlic, minced

6 Yukon gold potatoes (about 3 pounds), peeled and thinly sliced

1^1/$_2$ teaspoons kosher salt

Freshly ground black pepper

2^1/$_2$ cups heavy cream

PREHEAT THE OVEN TO 350°F. In a small bowl, using a fork, mash together the butter and garlic. Use 1 tablespoon of the garlic butter to grease a 12-inch (1^1/$_2$-quart) oval gratin dish.

LAYER ONE-THIRD OF THE POTATO SLICES, slightly over-lapping, in the prepared gratin dish. Sprinkle the potatoes with ^{1}/$_2$ teaspoon of the salt and a few grindings of pepper. Repeat with another one-third of the potato slices and another ^{1}/$_2$ teaspoon of the salt and a few grindings of pepper. End with the remaining potatoes, taking care to arrange them in an attractive pattern. Season with the remaining ^{1}/$_2$ teaspoon salt and pepper. Pour the cream over the top of the potatoes and dot with the remaining garlic butter.

PLACE THE GRATIN ON A STURDY BAKING SHEET lined with aluminum foil. Bake until the potatoes are tender when pierced with the tip of a thin-bladed knife and the top is a dark, golden brown, about 1^1/$_2$ hours. Let rest for 10 minutes before serving.

PORCINI MUSHROOM *and*
YELLOW FINN POTATO GRATIN

Serves 4 to 6 Porcini mushrooms are intensely flavored, meaty Italian mushrooms, also known as *cèpes*. They're hard to find fresh, and usually their Oregonian cousins don't have nearly as much flavor as the European variety. Dried Italian porcini, however, can be found in most specialty markets or well-stocked supermarkets. Although they might strike you as unreasonably expensive, it takes only an ounce or two to flavor a whole dish. To reconstitute any dried mushrooms, just soak them in warm water for 20 minutes. Save the soaking liquid, as it retains tons of mushroom flavor. Strain it through a fine-mesh sieve or coffee filter to remove any sand or grit. If you can't find Yellow Finn potatoes, any buttery potato, such as Yukon golds, will work just fine.

1 ounce dried porchini mushrooms

4 tablespoons unsalted butter, at room temperature

2 large cloves garlic, minced

1 yellow onion, finely chopped

8 ounces cremini or button mushrooms, thinly sliced

2 tablespoons chopped fresh flat-leaf parsley

1/2 teaspoon minced fresh thyme

4 Yellow Finn or Yukon gold potatoes (about 2 pounds), peeled and thinly sliced

1 cup heavy cream

Kosher salt and freshly ground black pepper

1/4 cup freshly grated Parmesan

IN A SMALL BOWL, COMBINE THE DRIED MUSHROOMS with enough water to just cover. Soak until softened, about 30 minutes. Remove the mushrooms from the soaking liquid and coarsely chop. Strain the soaking liquid through a fine-mesh sieve or coffee filter and reserve.

PREHEAT THE OVEN TO 350°F. In a small bowl, using a fork, mash together 2 tablespoons of the butter and half of the garlic. Use half of the garlic butter to grease an 8 by 11-inch (2-quart) gratin dish.

IN A MEDIUM SAUTÉ PAN, melt the remaining 2 tablespoons butter over medium-high heat. Add the onion and cook until translucent, 2 to 3 minutes. Add the remaining garlic and cook until fragrant, about 1 minute. Add the fresh mushrooms; cook until they have released their liquid and it has evaporated. Remove from the heat. Stir in the soaked mushrooms, parsley, and thyme; mix well.

ARRANGE ONE-HALF OF THE POTATO SLICES in the prepared gratin dish. Distribute the mushroom mixture evenly over the potatoes and layer the remaining potato slices over the top, taking care to arrange them in an attractive pattern.

IN A SMALL BOWL, COMBINE THE CREAM and $^1/_4$ cup of the reserved mushroom soaking liquid; reserve the remaining soaking liquid for another use. Pour the cream mixture over the gratin. Season with salt and pepper. Sprinkle the cheese evenly over the top and dot with the remaining garlic butter.

PLACE THE GRATIN ON A STURDY BAKING SHEET. Bake until the potatoes are tender when pierced with the tip of a knife and the top is golden and bubbly, about $1^1/_2$ hours. Let rest for 10 minutes before serving.

PROSCIUTTO-MASHED POTATO GRATIN

Serves 4 to 6 Prosciutto is an Italian ham that has been seasoned, salt cured, and air dried. Combined with mashed potatoes and cheese in this gratin, it makes a comfortingly tasty one-dish supper. Prosciutto varies in saltiness, so taste as you go before adding salt as needed. As you break into the soft ham-flavored mashed potatoes in this dish, you uncover the surprise of hot, gooey, melting mozzarella cheese. Serve with a fresh spinach salad dressed with a balsamic vinaigrette. The peppery flavor of arugula makes a great accompaniment, too.

6 russet potatoes (about 3 pounds), peeled and cut into quarters

¹/₂ cup unsalted butter, at room temperature

¹/₂ cup heavy cream

¹/₂ cup freshly grated Parmesan

2 large eggs

8 ounces very thinly sliced prosciutto, coarsely chopped

Kosher salt and freshly ground black pepper

Freshly grated nutmeg

8 ounces mozzarella, thickly sliced

Topping

¹/₂ cup fresh bread crumbs

¹/₂ cup coarsely chopped walnuts

¹/₂ cup freshly grated Parmesan

Freshly ground black pepper

3 tablespoons unsalted butter, melted

IN A LARGE SAUCEPAN, COMBINE THE POTATOES with cold water to cover and bring to a boil over high heat. Lower the heat to maintain a gentle boil and cook until very tender, about 25 minutes. Drain well and return the potatoes to the hot pan to dry out a little. Stir in the butter and cream and mash until smooth. Add the Parmesan, eggs, and prosciutto and beat with a wooden spoon until smooth. Season to taste with salt, pepper, and nutmeg.

PREHEAT THE OVEN TO 350°F. Generously butter a 12-inch oval (1¹/₂-quart) oval gratin dish.

TRANSFER HALF OF THE MASHED POTATO MIXTURE to the prepared gratin dish. Arrange the mozzarella slices over the potatoes. Spread the remaining mashed potato mixture evenly over the cheese.

TO MAKE THE TOPPING: In a medium bowl, combine the bread crumbs, walnuts, Parmesan, and pepper and toss to mix. Drizzle with the melted butter and toss until the bread crumbs have absorbed all of the butter.

SPRINKLE THE TOPPING EVENLY over the gratin. Place on a sturdy baking sheet. Bake until golden and crispy, about 30 minutes. Let rest for 5 minutes before serving.

BLUE CHEESE *and* STRAW POTATO GRATIN

Serves 4 to 6 It takes just three ingredients and very little time—especially if you grate the potatoes in a food processor—to make this blue cheese–studded, wonderfully crispy gratin. Work quickly once the potatoes are grated, as they will start to discolor immediately. Discard any liquid that's released. This is a great side dish, but it can also be served for lunch with a lightly dressed butter lettuce and tomato salad. Be sure that you cook the gratin until it's a dark golden brown; the super-crunchy bits at the edge are a special treat.

4 russet potatoes (about 2 pounds), peeled, rinsed, and dried

$^1/_2$ to $^3/_4$ cup freshly crumbled blue cheese, such as Maytag blue, Gorgonzola, or Stilton

Kosher salt

4 tablespoons unsalted butter, at room temperature

PREHEAT THE OVEN TO 400°F. Generously butter an 8 by 10-inch ($1^1/_2$-quart) gratin dish.

COARSELY GRATE THE POTATOES. Using your hands, gently squeeze out some of the excess liquid (it's okay if they are still damp). Transfer a generous one-half of the potatoes to the prepared gratin dish. Sprinkle the blue cheese evenly over the top. Cover with the remaining potatoes, season with salt, and dot the surface with the butter, spreading the butter over as much of the surface as possible. (The areas that are coated with butter will color and crisp.)

PLACE THE GRATIN ON A STURDY BAKING SHEET. Bake until really crusty and deep golden brown, 1 to $1^1/_2$ hours. Serve immediately.

LEMON-SCENTED SMOKED SALMON
and POTATO GRATIN

Serves 6 Decadent smoked salmon blends with the subtle scent of lemon and the silkiness of heavy cream to make a gratin that's wonderful for lunch or supper. Smoked, or Nova Scotia, salmon is cold-smoked from 1 day to up to 3 weeks. Lox has been brined first, then smoked. Either can be used here. Enjoy this dish with a well-chilled, crisp Sauvignon Blanc or floral Viognier.

1¹/₂ cups whole milk

1¹/₂ cups heavy cream

1 teaspoon freshly grated lemon zest

1 teaspoon kosher salt

Freshly ground black pepper

4 large Yukon gold potatoes (about 3 pounds), peeled and thickly sliced

8 ounces smoked salmon, thinly sliced

2 tablespoons unsalted butter

PREHEAT THE OVEN TO 375°F. Generously butter a 12-inch (1¹/₂-quart) oval gratin dish.

IN A LARGE SAUTÉ PAN, COMBINE THE MILK, cream, lemon zest, salt, and pepper to taste. Bring to a boil over medium heat. Add the potatoes and cook until they are just beginning to be tender but not fully cooked, about 12 minutes.

USING A SLOTTED SPOON, transfer half of the potato slices to the prepared gratin dish. Arrange the salmon over the potatoes. Arrange the remaining potato slices over the layer of salmon, taking care to arrange them in an attractive design. Pour the cream mixture over the top and dot with the butter.

PLACE THE GRATIN ON A STURDY BAKING SHEET. Bake until the potatoes are tender when pierced with the tip of a knife and the top is a dark, golden brown, 25 to 30 minutes. Let rest for 10 minutes before serving. Serve hot or warm.

NEW POTATO GRATIN *with* SOUR CREAM, CHIVES, *and* ONION

Serves 4 to 6 Baby fingerling potatoes, with their thin skins, don't need to be peeled, making this dish a cinch, especially if you have a metal gratin dish and can sauté the onion on the stove top. Although perhaps not as pretty as some of the other gratins in this book, the flavor is full and delicious. This dish makes a terrific accompaniment to ham or roasted meat.

1 tablespoon unsalted butter

1 tablespoon olive oil

1 yellow onion, chopped

1 clove garlic, thinly sliced

1 tablespoon all-purpose flour

2 cups chicken stock (page 10) or canned low-sodium broth

1 cup sour cream

1/4 cup minced fresh chives

Kosher salt and freshly ground black pepper

1 1/2 pounds fingerling potatoes

1 cup freshly grated Gruyère

Chopped fresh chives, for garnish

PREHEAT THE OVEN TO 350°F. In a 9-inch (1-quart) oval stainless steel, copper, or cast-iron gratin dish, melt the butter with the olive oil over medium heat. Add the onion and cook until translucent, 2 to 3 minutes. Add the garlic and flour and cook, stirring constantly, for 1 minute. Add the chicken stock and whisk until smooth, creamy, and thickened. Whisk in the sour cream and minced chives. Season to taste with salt and pepper. Add the potatoes, toss to mix, and spread the mixture evenly in the pan.

SPRINKLE THE CHEESE EVENLY OVER THE TOP. Place the gratin on a sturdy baking sheet. Bake until the potatoes are tender and the top is golden, about 50 minutes. Garnish with the chopped chives and serve immediately.

CUMIN-FLAVORED POTATOES *with* POBLANO CHILES *and* CILANTRO

Serves 6 Poblano chiles, sometimes incorrectly labeled as *pasilla*, are dark green triangular-shaped chiles with a distinctly rich flavor. They are usually mild to medium in spiciness, although occasionally a very fiery one slips through, so taste for heat as you assemble this dish. You can also increase the cumin by as much as another tablespoon if you really like its aromatic taste.

2 tablespoons olive oil

2 yellow onions, thinly sliced

$^1/_2$ teaspoon kosher salt

3 poblano chiles, roasted, peeled, seeded, and diced

1 tablespoon ground cumin

3 cloves garlic, thinly sliced

1 cup vegetable stock (page 11) or chicken stock (page 10)

1 cup heavy cream

Freshly ground black pepper

5 Yukon gold potatoes (about 2$^1/_2$ pounds), thinly sliced

$^1/_2$ cup chopped fresh cilantro

1$^1/_2$ cups freshly grated Monterey Jack

Fresh cilantro leaves, for garnish

PREHEAT THE OVEN TO 350°F. Generously coat a 12-inch (1$^1/_2$-quart) oval gratin dish with olive oil.

IN A MEDIUM SAUTÉ PAN, heat the olive oil over medium-high heat. Add the onions, sprinkle with the salt, and cook until translucent, 2 to 3 minutes. Add the chiles, cumin and garlic, and cook, stirring, about 3 minutes. Add the stock and cream and bring to a boil. Remove from the heat and season to taste with salt and pepper.

ARRANGE ONE-THIRD OF THE POTATOES in the bottom of the prepared gratin dish. Using a slotted spoon, remove one-half of the onion mixture from the cream and spread evenly over the potatoes. Sprinkle with one-half of the cilantro and one-third of the cheese. Repeat. End with the remaining potatoes, taking care to arrange them in an attractive pattern. Pour the cream mixture evenly over the potatoes—use the back of your slotted spoon to press down a bit on the potatoes to submerge them in the cream. Sprinkle the remaining cheese over the top.

PLACE THE GRATIN ON A STURDY BAKING SHEET lined with aluminum foil. Bake until the potatoes are tender when pierced with the tip of a knife and the top is golden and bubbly, about 1 hour and 20 minutes. Let rest for 10 minutes before serving. Garnish with the fresh cilantro leaves.

SUBLIME SUPPERS

FETTUCCINI *with* PROSCIUTTO *and* PEAS

Serves 4 to 6 Pasta is the original comfort food; there are times when nothing else will satisfy. This gratin includes pasta in a rhapsody of comfort foods: fettuccini, the bite of Parmesan, salty prosciutto, and a crispy crust. Served in individual gratin dishes, it makes an elegant supper.

1 pound dried fettuccini

1 tablespoon unsalted butter

1 yellow onion, finely chopped

4 ounces thinly sliced prosciutto, coarsely chopped

2 cups heavy cream

$^1/_2$ cup freshly grated Parmesan

8 ounces frozen petit peas, thawed

1 teaspoon freshly grated lemon zest

Kosher salt and freshly ground black pepper

Topping

1 cup fresh bread crumbs

1 cup freshly grated Parmesan

Kosher salt and freshly ground black pepper

PREHEAT THE BROILER. Generously butter an 8 by 11-inch (2-quart) gratin dish.

BRING A LARGE POT OF SALTED WATER TO A BOIL. Add the pasta and cook according to the package directions; drain well, reserving $^1/_2$ cup pasta cooking water, and set aside.

IN A LARGE SAUTÉ PAN, MELT THE BUTTER over medium heat. Add the onion and cook, stirring occasionally, until translucent and beginning to caramelize, about 5 minutes. Add the prosciutto and cook for 1 minute. Add the cream and bring to a boil. Remove from the heat; add the Parmesan and stir until melted. Stir in the peas and lemon zest and season to taste with salt and pepper. Add the pasta and the reserved water and toss to combine. Transfer to the prepared gratin dish and smooth the top.

TO MAKE THE TOPPING: In a small bowl, combine the bread crumbs and Parmesan; toss to mix. Season to taste with salt and pepper.

SPRINKLE THE TOPPING EVENLY over the gratin. Place on a sturdy baking sheet. Set under the broiler, about 4 inches from the heat source, and broil until the pasta is heated through and the topping is golden and crispy, about 8 minutes. Serve immediately.

MEDITERRANEAN PENNE GRATIN

Serves 4 to 6 This main-course dish packs a tangy punch with a Mediterranean mélange of toothsome pasta, salty feta, Kalamata olives, sweet roasted red peppers, and tart cherry tomatoes. They all come together in a creamy sauce fragranced with oregano.

8 ounces dried penne

2 tablespoons unsalted butter

1 yellow onion, minced

2 cloves garlic, minced

2 cups chicken stock (page 10) or canned low-sodium broth

1 cup heavy cream

5 ounces feta, crumbled

$^1/_2$ cup freshly grated Parmesan

2 tablespoons minced fresh oregano

1 teaspoon minced fresh thyme

2 red bell peppers, roasted, peeled, and thinly sliced (see Note on page 44)

$^1/_2$ to 1 cup Kalamata olives, pitted and coarsely chopped

1 pint small cherry tomatoes, halved

Topping

1 cup fresh bread crumbs

5 ounces feta, crumbled

$^1/_2$ cup pine nuts

1 tablespoon minced fresh oregano

2 tablespoons unsalted butter, melted

PREHEAT THE OVEN TO 375°F. Generously butter an 8 by 11-inch (2-quart) gratin dish.

BRING A LARGE POT OF SALTED WATER TO A BOIL. Add the pasta and cook according to the package directions; drain well and set aside.

IN A LARGE SAUTÉ PAN, MELT THE BUTTER over medium heat. Add the onion and cook, stirring occasionally, until translucent and beginning to caramelize, about 5 minutes. Add the garlic and cook until fragrant, about 1 minute. Add the stock and bring to a boil. Remove from the heat. Stir in the cream, feta, Parmesan, oregano, thyme, roasted peppers, olives, and tomatoes. Add the pasta and toss to combine. Transfer to the prepared gratin dish and smooth the top.

TO MAKE THE TOPPING: In a small bowl, combine the bread crumbs, feta, pine nuts, and oregano. Drizzle with the melted butter and toss until the bread crumbs have absorbed all of the butter.

SPRINKLE THE TOPPING EVENLY over the gratin. Place on a sturdy baking sheet. Bake until golden, about 30 minutes. Let rest for 5 minutes before serving.

NOTE: Some fetas are very salty, so taste before using; if it seems too salty, soak it in milk for 10 minutes, then drain and pat dry.

THREE-CHEESE CAULIFLOWER GRATIN

Serves 4 to 6 This classic gratin uses three cheeses in the sauce: Parmesan to give an intense cheesy flavor, Gruyère for its nutty overtones, and aged Cheddar for its creamy tang and silky texture. Be careful not to overcook the cauliflower, and make sure you drain it very well, or it will dilute the cheese sauce.

1 teaspoon kosher salt

2 bay leaves

1 cauliflower (about 2 pounds), cut into florets

3 tablespoons unsalted butter

1 small yellow onion, finely chopped

3 tablespoons all-purpose flour

1 1/2 cups whole milk

1/2 cup freshly grated Gruyère

1/2 cup freshly grated Cheddar

1/4 cup freshly grated Parmesan

1 tablespoon Dijon mustard

Kosher salt and freshly ground black pepper

Topping

1/2 cup fresh bread crumbs

1/4 cup freshly grated Cheddar

1/4 cup freshly grated Parmesan

Kosher salt and freshly ground black pepper

Chopped fresh flat-leaf parsley, for garnish

PREHEAT THE OVEN TO 400°F. Generously butter a 12-inch (1 1/2-quart) oval gratin dish.

BRING A LARGE POT OF WATER TO A BOIL over high heat. Add the salt, bay leaves, and cauliflower florets and cook until the florets are tender, about 8 minutes. Drain the cauliflower well and discard the bay leaves. Transfer to the prepared gratin dish.

IN A MEDIUM SAUCEPAN, MELT THE BUTTER over medium heat. Add the onion and cook until translucent, about 4 minutes. Add the flour and cook, stirring constantly, for 1 minute. Add the milk and bring to a boil; cook, whisking constantly, until the sauce thickens, about 2 minutes. Remove from the heat. Stir in the Gruyère, Cheddar, Parmesan, and mustard. Season to taste with salt and pepper. Pour the sauce over the cauliflower.

TO MAKE THE TOPPING: In a small bowl, combine the bread crumbs, Cheddar, and Parmesan. Season to taste with salt and pepper.

SPRINKLE THE TOPPING EVENLY over the gratin. Place on a sturdy baking sheet. Bake until bubbly, about 15 minutes. Set under the broiler, about 4 inches from the heat source, and broil until golden, 3 to 5 minutes. Garnish with the parsley and serve immediately.

POTATO-PARMESAN GNOCCHI GRATIN

Serves 4   Gnocchi are Italian dumplings made of flour and potatoes or ricotta cheese. The tender little morsels are thimble sized and typically scored with fine ridges or indentations designed to hold the sauce. They're easy to make, although somewhat time-consuming. That being so, take advantage of good-quality, store-bought gnocchi, if necessary; excellent versions can be found in the refrigerator section of Italian markets and well-stocked supermarkets. If you use purchased gnocchi, this gratin can be made in minutes; just don't overcook the gnocchi, or they will bake up gooey instead of crisp and chewy. If you have time, though, make your own with the recipe on page 71; it's a rewarding process.

¹/₂ cup unsalted butter

4 cloves garlic, minced

6 tablespoons chopped fresh sage

2 (12-ounce) packages Parmesan gnocchi or Parmesan-Potato Gnocchi (recipe follows)

2 cups fresh bread crumbs

Kosher salt and freshly ground black pepper

Fresh sage leaves, cut into chiffonade, for garnish

PREHEAT THE OVEN TO 350°F. Generously butter an 8 by 11-inch (2-quart) gratin dish.

IN A MEDIUM SAUTÉ PAN, melt the butter over medium-high heat. Add the garlic and cook for 1 minute. Remove from the heat; add the sage and let infuse for 5 minutes.

IF USING PURCHASED GNOCCHI, bring a large pot of salted water to a boil. Add the gnocchi and cook according to the package directions. If using homemade, see the cooking instructions on the next page. Drain the gnocchi and place in the prepared gratin dish.

DRIZZLE HALF OF THE GARLIC-SAGE BUTTER over the gnocchi and toss to mix. Add the bread crumbs to the remaining garlic-sage butter in the pan and toss until the bread crumbs have absorbed all of the butter. Season to taste with salt and pepper. Sprinkle evenly over the top of the gratin.

PLACE THE GRATIN ON A STURDY BAKING SHEET. Bake until the top is golden and crispy, about 30 minutes. Garnish with the sage leaf chiffonade. Serve immediately.

POTATO-PARMESAN GNOCCHI

For light, tender gnocchi, use freshly baked russet potatoes, because their low moisture content requires less flour. Alternatively, you can boil the potatoes in lightly salted water until very tender. Forming the gnocchi takes a bit of practice, especially if you have the traditional wooden paddle used to make the grooves. If you don't, simply use the tines of a fork. It's a good idea to test-cook one gnocchi to see if you have added enough flour to your dough so that they hold together.

4 russet potatoes (about 2 pounds)

1 large egg, lightly beaten

$^1/_2$ cup freshly grated Parmesan

$1^1/_4$ to 2 cups all-purpose flour

$^1/_2$ teaspoon kosher salt

PREHEAT THE OVEN TO 350°F. Line a large baking sheet with parchment paper.

PRICK THE POTATOES WITH A FORK A FEW TIMES. Place on the oven rack and bake until completely tender, 40 minutes to 1 hour, depending on their size. Halve the potatoes and, using a small spoon, scoop out the hot potato flesh. Press through a potato ricer into a large bowl, or place in a bowl and mash until smooth with a potato masher.

MAKE A WELL IN THE CENTER OF THE POTATOES AND ADD THE EGG, Parmesan, $1^1/_4$ cups of the flour, and the salt. Using a fork, gradually stir the potatoes into the contents of the well, pulling them in from the sides, until all the ingredients are combined. Knead the mixture until it forms a soft, smooth dough. Continue adding flour $^1/_4$ cup at a time until the dough holds together and is no longer sticky. Turn out onto a lightly floured work surface. Divide the dough into 8 to 10 portions; roll each portion into a rope $^1/_2$ inch thick. Cut each rope into 1-inch pieces.

TO MAKE THE TRADITIONAL GROOVES ON YOUR GNOCCHI, gently press the tines of a fork into the top of a dumpling—as if trying to squash a pea—and with very gentle pressure, push the gnocchi away from you, rolling the gnocchi about a half turn and lifting the pressure on the fork as you finish. The fork will leave little grooves. Transfer to the prepared baking sheet. (It may take a few tries to get the pressure and rolling technique down; be patient while you get the hang of it, and reroll the gnocchi for another attempt if necessary.) Repeat with the remaining gnocchi. Let dry at room temperature for about 1 hour.

BRING A LARGE POT OF SALTED WATER TO A BOIL; lower the heat to maintain a simmer. Add a handful of the gnocchi and cook until they float back up to the surface. Using a slotted spoon, immediately transfer to a bowl. Repeat to cook the remaining gnocchi.

POLENTA *and* PORTOBELLO MUSHROOM GRATIN

Serves 4 to 6 Polenta, a coarse grind of cornmeal, was introduced to Italy from the Americas in the seventeenth century. Polenta was originally the food of the poor, but today it's eaten all over northern Europe and the United States. Many traditions call for cooking it to such stiffness that you can stand a spoon in it, but soft polenta, as in this recipe, is another popular preparation. In this gratin, ricotta cheese is added for a creamy, soft texture and fresh corn supplies crunch and a touch of sweetness. With portobello mushrooms, the giants of the mushroom world, it makes a more substantial meal. Substitute cremini or button mushrooms if you can't find portobellos. You can also make the polenta and simply top it with a drizzle of cream and a sprinkling of extra cheese for a very simple side dish.

4 cups water

1¹/₂ teaspoons kosher salt, plus more to taste

1 cup polenta (not instant)

2 tablespoons unsalted butter

1¹/₂ cups (16 ounces) ricotta

1 cup freshly grated provolone

1 cup freshly grated Parmesan

2 cups fresh corn kernels (about 3 ears) or 8 ounces frozen corn, thawed

Freshly ground black pepper

PREHEAT THE OVEN TO 375°F. Generously butter a 12-inch (1¹/₂-quart) oval gratin dish.

TO MAKE POLENTA: in a large saucepan, combine the water and 1¹/₂ teaspoons salt and bring to a boil over high heat. Add the polenta in a very slow, steady stream, whisking constantly. Cook, still whisking constantly, until thickened and bubbly, 10 to 15 minutes. (Take care, as the polenta can splutter as it thickens.) Remove from heat and add the butter, ricotta, provolone, and Parmesan and mix until smooth. Stir in the corn and season to taste with salt and pepper. Transfer to the prepared gratin dish.

IN A LARGE SAUTÉ PAN, melt 2 tablespoons of the butter with 2 tablespoons of the olive oil over medium-high heat. Add the mushrooms and cook, turning with tongs as needed, until tender and beginning to caramelize on both sides, about 4 minutes. Using the tongs, arrange the mushrooms on top of the polenta.

3 tablespoons unsalted butter

3 tablespoons olive oil

1 pound portobello mushrooms, and thickly sliced

1 yellow onion, minced

1 red bell pepper, cored, seeded, and thinly sliced

2 cloves garlic, minced

1 cup dry white wine

1 (15-ounce) can crushed tomatoes

1 teaspoon sugar

1 tablespoon minced fresh oregano

Kosher salt and freshly ground black pepper

1 cup freshly grated provolone

IN THE SAME PAN, melt the remaining 1 tablespoon butter and 1 tablespoon olive oil over medium-high heat. Add the onion and cook until translucent, 2 to 3 minutes. Add the bell pepper and cook until tender, about 5 minutes. Add the garlic, wine, tomatoes, and sugar and cook until reduced slightly and beginning to thicken. Stir in the oregano. Season to taste with salt and pepper.

SPOON THE TOMATO MIXTURE OVER THE TOP of the mushrooms and sprinkle with the provolone. Place the gratin on a sturdy baking sheet. Bake until bubbly and the cheese is melted and golden, 20 to 30 minutes. Serve immediately.

SAUSAGE, WHITE BEAN, *and* CHARD GRATIN

Serves 4 to 6 As your serving spoon breaks through the crust of this gratin, take a deep breath and inhale the fragrant aromas of fennel, creamy white beans, savory sausage, and earthy chard. This satisfying one-dish meal can be assembled ahead and baked just before serving. Then all you need to do is make a green salad, open a bottle of red wine, sit down with friends, and dig in.

3 mild Italian sausages (about 12 ounces), casings removed

1 yellow onion, thinly sliced

1/2 fennel bulb, thinly sliced

3 cloves garlic, thinly sliced

1 tablespoon fresh sage leaves, cut into chiffonade

1/2 to 1 teaspoon fennel seeds

Pinch of red pepper flakes

1 bunch white card, stems and leaves kept separate, cut into 1/4-inch slices

1 cup chicken stock (page 10) or canned low-sodium broth

2 (15-ounce) cans cannellini beans, rinsed and drained

1/2 cup sun-dried tomatoes, sliced

Kosher salt and freshly ground black pepper

1/4 cup freshly grated Parmesan

2 tablespoons freshly grated Gruyère

Topping

2 tablespoons olive oil

1/2 cup fresh bread crumbs

Freshly ground black pepper

PREHEAT THE OVEN TO 350°F. Lightly oil a 9-inch (1 1/2 quart) square gratin dish.

HEAT A LARGE SAUTÉ PAN OVER HIGH HEAT. Crumble in the sausage and cook, breaking up the lumps with a spatula, until golden brown, about 5 minutes. Using a slotted spoon, transfer the sausage to a small bowl.

POUR OFF ALL BUT 2 TABLESPOONS OF THE FAT in the pan. Return the pan to medium-high heat and add the onion; cook until translucent, about 5 minutes. Add the fresh fennel, garlic, sage, fennel seeds, and red pepper flakes and cook until the vegetables are softened, about 5 minutes. Add the chard stems and cook for 1 minute. Add the chard leaves and stock and cook for 1 minute. Remove from the heat. Stir in the beans and sun-dried tomatoes. Season to taste with salt and pepper. Transfer to the prepared gratin dish. Sprinkle the cheeses over the top.

TO MAKE THE TOPPING: In a small sauté pan, heat the olive oil over high heat. Add the bread crumbs and cook until golden brown, 2 to 3 minutes. Season to taste with pepper.

SPRINKLE THE TOPPING OVER THE GRATIN. Place on a sturdy baking sheet. Bake until deep, golden brown and bubbly, 30 to 40 minutes. Let rest for 10 minutes before serving.

CHICKEN POT GRATIN

Serves 4 to 6 This twist on an old standard is perfect comfort food—rich, creamy (since chicken thighs retain their moistness when poached), and easy to prepare ahead. This versatile dish is a hit at potlucks, and it freezes well, too.

3 cups chicken stock (page 10) or canned low-sodium broth

1 cup dry white wine

2 to 2¼ pounds boneless, skinless chicken thighs, cut into bite-sized pieces

3 carrots, peeled and thinly sliced

¼ cup unsalted butter

1 large yellow onion, finely chopped

3 celery stalks, finely chopped

2 large cloves garlic, minced

¼ cup all-purpose flour

1 teaspoon kosher salt

½ teaspoon freshly ground black pepper

8 ounces frozen petit peas, thawed

¼ cup chopped fresh flat-leaf parsley

2 tablespoons minced fresh thyme

IN A LARGE PAN, COMBINE THE STOCK AND WINE and bring to a boil over high heat. Add the chicken thighs and carrots and return to a boil. Lower the heat and simmer until tender, about 15 minutes. Remove from the heat and let the chicken and carrots cool in the cooking liquid for at least 20 minutes—you can even cook them the night before and refrigerate them in the broth overnight. Using a slotted spoon, transfer the chicken and carrots to an 8 by 11-inch (2-quart) gratin dish; reserve the cooking liquid.

PREHEAT THE OVEN TO 350°F. In a large saucepan, melt the butter over medium heat. Add the onion and celery and cook until translucent, about 4 minutes. Add the garlic and cook until fragrant, about 2 minutes. Sprinkle in the flour and cook, stirring constantly, for 2 minutes. Add 2 cups of the reserved chicken cooking liquid and bring to a boil. Cook, whisking constantly, until the sauce thickens, about 2 minutes. Whisk in the salt and pepper. Stir in the peas, parsley, and thyme. Pour the pea mixture over the chicken and carrots.

Topping

2 cups fresh bread crumbs

1 cup freshly grated Parmesan

1/4 cup minced fresh flat-leaf parsley

1 clove garlic, minced

1 teaspoon herbes de Provence

3 tablespoons unsalted butter, melted

Kosher salt and freshly ground black pepper

TO MAKE THE TOPPING: In a medium bowl, combine the bread crumbs, Parmesan, parsley, garlic, and herbes de Provence; toss to mix. Drizzle with the melted butter and toss until the bread crumbs have absorbed all of the butter. Season to taste with salt and pepper.

SPRINKLE THE TOPPING EVENLY over the gratin. Place on a sturdy baking sheet. Bake until the surface is bubbly, golden, and crisp, about 40 minutes. Let rest for 10 minutes before serving.

MEXICAN SHREDDED PORK GRATIN

Serves 4 to 6 The tomatillo is known by many names, including Mexican green tomato, tomato verde, and Chinese lantern plants. Tomatillos, from the nightshade family, look like green tomatoes covered with a thin, papery husk. Choose firm fruits with clean, close-fitting husks. Peel away the husks and rinse off the waxy residue underneath under warm running water before using. Fresh tomatillos are not always available, but canned are an excellent substitute. The pork can be cooked a day or two ahead to make this dish even easier to assemble.

2 to 2¹/₂ pounds pork shoulder

2 tablespoons vegetable oil

1 large yellow onion, thinly sliced

3 cloves garlic, minced

2 (10-ounce) cans tomatillos, drained and coarsely chopped

2 to 3 serrano or jalapeño chiles, seeded and minced

¹/₄ cup chopped fresh cilantro

2 teaspoons kosher salt

Freshly ground black pepper

1¹/₂ cups freshly grated Monterey Jack

1¹/₂ cups freshly grated sharp Cheddar

IN A LARGE SAUCEPAN, COMBINE THE PORK with cold water just to cover. Bring to a boil over high heat, skimming off and discarding any foam as it rises to the top. Lower the heat and simmer, covered, until the meat is very tender and almost ready to fall apart, about 2 hours. Remove from the heat and let the meat cool in the cooking liquid. When cool enough to handle, transfer the meat to a bowl and shred, discarding any fat; reserve the cooking liquid.

PREHEAT THE OVEN TO 400°F. Lightly oil a 12-inch (1¹/₂-quart) oval gratin dish. In a large sauté pan, heat the oil over medium heat. Add the onion and cook, stirring occasionally, until beginning to caramelize, about 5 minutes. Add the garlic, tomatillos, and chiles and cook, stirring, for 2 minutes. Add ¹/₂ cup of the reserved pork cooking liquid and cook until thickened and reduced by one-half. Remove from the heat and stir in the cilantro, salt, and the shredded pork. Season with pepper to taste.

TRANSFER THE PORK MIXTURE to the prepared gratin dish. Sprinkle the cheeses over the top. Place the gratin on a sturdy baking sheet. Bake until the top is bubbly and the cheese is melted and golden, about 30 minutes. Let rest for 5 minutes before serving.

GRATINÉED SAVORY RICE PUDDING
with VEGETABLES

Serves 6 to 8 This savory rice custard harbors cubes of root vegetables or squash and makes an ultimately satisfying dish. Parsnips, turnips, carrots, rutabaga, and/or butternut squash can be used in any combination. They add a wonderful touch of sweetness to this dish. It can be served alone or as an accompaniment to grilled meat or fish.

Topping

1 cup crushed croutons

1/2 cup freshly grated Parmesan

1 teaspoon minced fresh thyme

2 tablespoons olive oil

1 yellow onion, minced

3 large cloves garlic, minced

2 pounds mixed root vegetables, peeled and cut into 1/2-inch dice

Kosher salt and freshly ground black pepper

1 1/2 cups vegetable stock (page 11) or water

3 large eggs

1 cup heavy cream

2 cups cooked, cooled, long-grain rice

1 cup ricotta

1 cup freshly grated mozzarella

1/2 cup freshly grated Parmesan

PREHEAT THE OVEN TO 350°F. Generously butter an 8 by 11-inch (2-quart) gratin dish. In a small bowl, combine the croutons, Parmesan, and thyme; set aside.

IN A MEDIUM SAUTÉ PAN, heat the olive oil over medium-high heat. Add the onion and cook until translucent, 2 to 3 minutes. Add the garlic and cook 3 minutes. Add the root vegetables and cook 2 minutes. Season generously with salt and pepper. Add the stock and bring to a boil. Lower the heat and simmer, covered, until just tender, about 10 minutes. Set aside for 5 minutes to cool a little.

IN LARGE BOWL, WHISK TOGETHER THE EGGS and cream. Stir in the rice, ricotta, mozzarella, and Parmesan. Add one cup of the hot vegetable mixture and stir to temper the eggs. Add the remaining vegetable mixture, stirring until combined. Transfer to the prepared gratin dish.

PLACE THE GRATIN ON A STURDY BAKING SHEET. Bake until the edges are set, but the center is still very loose, 20 minutes. Remove from the oven and stir well. Smooth the top, sprinkle the bread-crumb mixture evenly over the gratin, and return to the oven. Bake until the custard is just set and the top is golden, 15 to 20 minutes. Let rest for 5 minutes before serving.

ELEGANT MAINS

Zucchini Boats with Mushrooms
and Fontina

Cheddar Gratinéed Seabass

Seafood Gratin

Halibut Gratin with Coconut Sauce

Sesame-Topped Jade Salmon Gratin

Piccata Chicken Gratin

Emmenthaler Chicken Breasts

Lamb and Eggplant Gratin with
North African Spices

Lamb Chop Cassoulet

ZUCCHINI BOATS *with* MUSHROOMS *and* FONTINA

Serves 4 to 6 This attractive vegetable main dish features zucchini boats filled with savory mushrooms and gratinéed under a layer of Italy's famed fontina cheese. Look for the original fontina, labeled *Val d'Aosta*. Other versions just don't seem to look, taste, or melt the same way. *Duxelles* is the French name for a mixture of finely chopped mushrooms, well seasoned and sautéed in butter. Choose small, firm zucchini, which have minimal seeds, for this dish.

6 zucchini (about 1 1/2 pounds)

2 tablespoons unsalted butter

1 yellow onion, minced

8 ounces button mushrooms, finely chopped

2 tablespoons dry sherry

1 large tomato, peeled, seeded, coarsely chopped

3 tablespoons minced fresh flat-leaf parsley

1 teaspoon minced fresh thyme

Kosher salt and freshly ground black pepper

8 ounces fontina cheese, preferably Val d'Aosta, thinly sliced

TRIM AND HALVE THE ZUCCHINI. Using a teaspoon, remove any seeds and create a channel about 1/2 inch deep down the center.

BRING A LARGE POT OF SALTED WATER TO A BOIL. Add the zucchini and cook just until crisp-tender, about 2 minutes. Using tongs, carefully transfer the zucchini, cut sides down, to a fine-mesh sieve. Rinse under cold water to stop the cooking. Drain well and place, cut sides down, on paper towels to drain completely.

PREHEAT THE BROILER. Butter a 9 by 13-inch (3-quart) gratin dish.

IN A LARGE SAUTÉ PAN, melt the butter over medium heat. Add the onion and cook until translucent, 2 to 3 minutes. Add the mushrooms and cook, stirring occasionally, until their liquid has evaporated. Add the sherry and cook until evaporated. Stir in the tomato, parsley, and thyme. Season to taste with salt and pepper.

TRANSFER THE ZUCCHINI to the prepared gratin dish. Divide the filling among the zucchini and cover with the fontina slices. Place the gratin dish on a sturdy baking sheet. Set under the broiler, about 4 inches from the heat source, and broil until the cheese is golden and bubbly, about 5 minutes. Serve immediately.

CHEDDAR GRATINÉED SEA BASS

Serves 6 Mild-flavored sea bass works well in dishes with distinctive flavors. Here, blanketed with a golden topping of sharp aged Cheddar, grainy mustard, and cream, it creates its own sauce as it bakes. Traditionally this dish is made with cod, a European favorite, but declining catches have made the right kind of cod difficult to find, and so the sea bass stands delicately in its stead. For the cheese, look for aged Cheddar with an assertive bite; it will add lots of flavor and melt beautifully. Try this dish served with boiled new potatoes and garden peas.

6 sea bass fillets (about 6 ounces each, at least 1 inch thick)

Kosher salt and freshly ground black pepper

2 cups freshly grated sharp Cheddar

3 tablespoons heavy cream

1 tablespoon whole-grain mustard

Pinch of cayenne pepper

Paprika, for garnish

PREHEAT THE OVEN TO 350°F. Generously butter a gratin dish just large enough to hold the sea bass with about $^1/_2$ inch of space between the fillets.

RINSE THE FILLETS AND PAT DRY WITH PAPER TOWELS. Arrange in the prepared gratin dish and season with salt and pepper.

IN A SMALL BOWL, COMBINE THE CHEESE, cream, mustard, and cayenne; mix well. Divide the topping evenly among the fillets, mounding it on top of each.

PLACE THE GRATIN ON A STURDY BAKING SHEET. Bake until the fish is opaque throughout and the top is golden and bubbly, 20 to 25 minutes. If the fish is cooked through but the top isn't brown enough, heat the broiler, set the gratin under it, about 4 inches from the heat source, and broil, until deeply golden. Dust the top with paprika. Serve immediately, spooning up the pan juices around the fish.

SEAFOOD GRATIN

Serve 6   This is a truly decadent dish, worthy of celebration—and well worth the time it takes to prepare. Choose small, black mussels for the best flavor. Store mussels, a bivalve shellfish, in a lightly covered bowl in the refrigerator, never in a sealed plastic bag, as they will suffocate. Large sea scallops, also bivalves (as well as smaller bay scallops), are rarely found in the shell in the United States, but a good fishmonger provides them freshly shucked. Cook scallops very gently for a short time to retain their delicate texture. This gratin can be served in individual dishes for an elegant presentation, either alone or on a bed of silky mashed potatoes.

2 pounds mussels, scrubbed and debearded

1 cup dry white wine

12 ounces (about 18) medium shrimp, peeled, deveined, and halved lengthwise

8 ounces sea scallops, halved crosswise

4 tablespoons unsalted butter

1 pound leeks, trimmed, washed, and thinly sliced (see Note on page 47)

$^1/_4$ cup all-purpose flour

$^1/_2$ cup crème fraîche

2 tablespoons freshly squeezed lemon juice

PREHEAT THE OVEN TO 450°F. Generously butter an 8 by 10-inch ($1^1/_2$-quart) gratin dish.

DISCARD ANY MUSSELS WITH BROKEN SHELLS or that do not close to the touch. In a large sauté pan, combine the mussels and wine over medium-high heat. Bring to a boil. Cover and cook, shaking the pan frequently, for 5 minutes. Transfer the mussels to a bowl as they open. When all the mussels are cooked and cool enough to handle, remove the meats to a bowl. Discard the shells, reserving the liquid in the pan.

STRAIN THE PAN JUICES through a fine-mesh sieve or coffee filter, return to the pan, and bring to a boil. Add the shrimp and scallops and cook until the shrimp are just beginning to turn pink and curl and the scallops are just losing their transparency, 2 to 3 minutes. Do not overcook—they will finish cooking in the sauce. Transfer the shrimp and scallops to the bowl with the mussels. Transfer the cooking liquid to a small bowl and set aside.

continued

SEAFOOD GRATIN *continued*

Kosher salt and freshly ground
black pepper

Topping

2 tablespoons unsalted butter

$^1/_2$ cup fresh bread crumbs

Kosher salt and freshly ground
black pepper

IN THE SAME PAN, MELT 2 TABLESPOONS OF THE BUTTER over medium-high heat. Add the leeks and cook until very tender, about 5 minutes. Add the remaining butter. When the butter is melted, add the flour and cook, whisking constantly, for 1 minute. Add the reserved cooking liquid and bring to a boil, whisking constantly. Cook for 1 minute. Add the crème fraîche and lemon juice and whisk until smooth. Season to taste with salt and pepper. Add the cooked seafood and stir gently until combined. Transfer the seafood mixture to the prepared gratin dish.

TO MAKE THE TOPPING: In a small sauté pan, melt the butter over medium-high heat. Add the bread crumbs and toss until they have absorbed all of the butter. Continue cooking, stirring constantly, until lightly browned and crispy. Remove from the heat and season to taste with salt and pepper.

SPRINKLE THE TOPPING EVENLY over the gratin. (If you want to be a little extravagant, drizzle more crème fraîche over the top of the sauced seafood before you add the topping.)

PLACE THE GRATIN ON A STURDY BAKING SHEET. Bake until bubbly and golden, about 5 minutes. If the seafood is warmed throughout but the top isn't brown enough, heat the broiler, set the gratin under it, about 4 inches from the heat source, and broil until deeply golden; but watch carefully to avoid overcooking. Serve immediately, or let rest until warm.

HALIBUT GRATIN *with* COCONUT SAUCE

Serves 6   Halibut is a firm-fleshed, mild-flavored white fish that lends itself well to the Asian flavors in this sauce. Unsweetened coconut cream is drawn from canned unsweetened coconut milk, found in Asian or other specialty food stores—do not confuse it with packages labeled "light" or with sweetened cream of coconut, used primarily for desserts and tropical drinks. Let the can of coconut milk sit for a couple of days to allow the rich cream to separate from the thin milk and float to the top. Spoon off the rich, thick cream and follow the recipe. Do not shake the can!

6 halibut steaks (6 ounces each), about $2^1/2$ inches thick

1 cup unsweetened coconut cream (from a 13-ounce can of coconut milk)

2 stalks lemongrass, bottom 3 inches only, finely minced

2 teaspoons freshly grated lime zest

1 small clove garlic, minced

1 or 2 bird's-eye or serrano chiles, seeded and finely minced

1 tablespoon Thai fish sauce

$^1/4$ cup firmly packed fresh basil leaves, cut into chiffonade

$^1/4$ cup firmly packed fresh mint leaves, chopped

Topping

1 cup fresh bread crumbs

$^1/4$ cup sesame seeds

2 tablespoons vegetable oil

1 teaspoon toasted sesame oil

Kosher salt and freshly ground black pepper

PREHEAT THE OVEN TO 350°F. Generously butter a gratin dish just large enough to hold the halibut with about $^1/2$ inch of space in between the steaks.

IN A SMALL SAUCEPAN, COMBINE THE COCONUT CREAM, lemongrass, lime zest, garlic, chile(s), and fish sauce and bring just to a boil over medium heat. Remove from the heat and stir in the basil and mint; set aside.

TO MAKE THE TOPPING: In a small bowl, combine the bread crumbs and sesame seeds. Drizzle the vegetable and sesame oils over the bread-crumb mixture and toss until the bread crumbs have absorbed all of the oil. Season to taste with salt and pepper.

RINSE THE HALIBUT and pat dry with paper towels. Arrange in the prepared gratin dish. Spoon the sauce evenly over the halibut and sprinkle the topping evenly over the top. Place the gratin on a sturdy baking sheet. Bake until the topping is golden and the fish is opaque throughout, 30 to 40 minutes. Serve immediately.

SESAME-TOPPED JADE SALMON GRATIN

Serves 4 to 6   Jade green is the color of the thick, piquant sauce in this dish, made with fresh cilantro and parsley. The vibrant color of the herbs contrasts with the pink of the salmon, and their tangy flavor counters its oiliness. Fillets, about 1¹/₂ inches thick are topped with the rich flavor of toasted sesame oil–coated bread crumbs and laced with sesame seeds. Salmon not only tastes great, it's good for you, rich in omega-3 fatty acids, an important component of a healthy diet. Serve with jasmine rice, and spoon any extra sauce on the side.

1 cup firmly packed fresh cilantro leaves

1 cup firmly packed fresh flat-leaf parsley leaves

2 green onions, coarsely chopped

¹/₂ cup walnut halves, toasted

1 clove garlic, chopped

¹/₂ jalepeño chile, seeded and minced

¹/₃ cup vegetable oil

1 to 2 tablespoons freshly squeezed lemon juice

Kosher salt and freshly ground black pepper

Topping

¹/₂ cup fresh bread crumbs

¹/₄ cup sesame seeds

1 tablespoon vegetable oil

1 teaspoon toasted sesame oil

Kosher salt and freshly ground black pepper

4 to 6 salmon fillets (6 ounces each)

PREHEAT THE OVEN TO 350°F. Generously oil a gratin dish just large enough to hold the salmon with about ¹/₂-inch of space in between the fillets.

IN THE BOWL OF A FOOD PROCESSOR, combine the cilantro, parsley, green onions, walnuts, garlic, and some of the chile and process until finely chopped. With the motor running, drizzle in the vegetable oil and process until smooth. Season to taste with the lemon juice, salt, pepper, and the remaining chile.

TO MAKE THE TOPPING: In a small bowl, combine the bread crumbs and sesame seeds. Drizzle the vegetable and sesame oils over the bread crumbs and toss until the bread crumbs have absorbed all of the oil. Season with salt and pepper to taste.

RINSE THE SALMON AND PAT DRY WITH PAPER TOWELS. Arrange in the prepared gratin dish. Spoon enough sauce over the fillets to coat and sprinkle the topping evenly over the top. Place the gratin on a sturdy baking sheet. Bake until the topping is golden and the fish is opaque throughout, about 20 minutes. For a really golden crust, finish the salmon under the broiler, about 4 inches from the heat source. Serve immediately with any extra sauce.

PICCATA CHICKEN GRATIN

Serves 4 to 6 Marinating chicken thighs in a mixture of garlic, herbs, olive oil, and a little lemon juice adds loads of flavor. The lemon slices in this dish cook under the chicken, loosing their acidity as they caramelize and add dimension. The piquant flavors of lemon and capers in the topping contrast with the chicken to make an elegant dish that can be served as a family dinner or easily multiplied for a crowd. Serve the chicken on a bed of sautéed kale or other greens. Spoon the sauce from the pan over the top and arrange the soft-cooked lemons around the plate.

6 skinless chicken thighs

4 large cloves garlic, minced

2 tablespoons olive oil

1 tablespoon freshly squeezed lemon juice

2 teaspoons minced fresh rosemary

1 teaspoon minced fresh thyme

1 lemon, thinly sliced

1 cup chicken stock (page 10) or canned low-sodium broth

Kosher salt and freshly ground black pepper

Topping

1/2 cup fresh bread crumbs

1 tablespoon minced fresh flat-leaf parsley

1 teaspoon minced fresh thyme

1 teaspoon minced fresh rosemary

1 tablespoon capers, drained

1 teaspoon freshly grated lemon zest

2 tablespoons olive oil

TRIM THE CHICKEN THIGHS of any fat and place in a sealable plastic bag. Add the garlic, olive oil, lemon juice rosemary, thyme, and pepper. Toss the bag to coat the chicken. Set aside to marinate for 1 hour or refrigerate overnight.

PREHEAT THE OVEN TO 350°F. Lightly oil an 8 by 11-inch (2-quart) gratin dish.

ARRANGE THE LEMON SLICES over the bottom of the prepared gratin dish. Remove the chicken from the bag and arrange the thighs on top so that they are about 1/2 inch apart. Pour the stock over and season with salt and pepper.

SET THE GRATIN ON A STURDY BAKING SHEET. Bake until the chicken is cooked through and the chicken stock has reduced by one half, about 45 minutes.

MEANWHILE, MAKE THE TOPPING: In a small bowl, combine the bread crumbs, parsley, thyme, rosemary, capers, and lemon zest. Drizzle with the olive oil and toss until the bread crumbs have absorbed all of the oil.

REMOVE THE GRATIN FROM THE OVEN. Sprinkle the topping evenly over the chicken, return to the oven, and continue baking until the topping is golden and crispy, about 20 minutes longer. Serve immediately.

EMMENTHALER CHICKEN BREASTS

Serves 6 Here's a dish that's pure comfort food and yet also elegant enough for company. In this preparation, the chicken is first poached and then cooled in the poaching liquid for added flavor. If serving for company, make the chicken, sauce, and a salad ahead; that way you'll have plenty of time to enjoy your guests. Serve the gratin with fresh noodles tossed in a little butter and plenty of freshly ground black pepper.

4 thick slices bacon, cut into
$^1/_4$-inch dice

1 yellow onion, thinly sliced

1 carrot, peeled and thinly sliced

1 celery stalk, thinly sliced

1 cup dry white wine

3 cups chicken stock (page 10) or
canned low-sodium broth

1 bay leaf, 1 sprig fresh thyme, and
6 sprigs fresh flat-leaf parsley tied
to make a bouquet garni

6 boneless, skinless chicken breast
halves (about 6 ounces each)

$^1/_4$ cup unsalted butter

$^1/_4$ cup all-purpose flour

$^1/_2$ cup half-and-half

1 cup freshly grated Emmenthaler,
plus extra for sprinkling

1 tablespoon Dijon mustard

Kosher salt and freshly ground
black pepper

Fresh flat-leaf parsley leaves,
for garnish

LIGHTLY OIL A 12-INCH ($1^1/_2$-quart) oval gratin dish. In a large sauté pan, cook the bacon over medium heat until just beginning to brown, about 3 minutes. Add the onion and cook until translucent, about 3 minutes. Add the carrot and celery; cook until just beginning to soften, about 4 minutes. Add the wine, stock, bouquet garni, and chicken breasts and bring to a boil. Lower the heat and simmer very gently until the chicken is opaque throughout, 15 to 20 minutes. Remove from the heat, cover, and let sit in the hot liquid for 30 minutes.

TRANSFER THE CHICKEN BREASTS to the prepared gratin dish; set aside. Pour the cooking liquid through a fine-mesh sieve; set aside 2 cups of the cooking liquid. Reserve the remaining cooking liquid and vegetables for another use.

PREHEAT THE BROILER. In a medium saucepan, melt the butter over medium heat. Add the flour and cook, whisking constantly, until the flour takes on a straw color. Whisk in the half-and-half and the 2 cups reserved cooking liquid and bring to a boil. Cook, whisking constantly, for 1 minute. Remove from the heat and stir in the cheese and mustard. Season to taste with salt and pepper. Pour the cheese sauce evenly over the chicken and sprinkle with additional cheese.

PLACE THE GRATIN ON A STURDY BAKING SHEET. Set under the broiler, about 4 inches from the heat source, and broil until golden and bubbly, about 8 minutes. Garnish the gratin with the parsley and serve immediately.

CHÈVRE-TOPPED LENTIL SOUP

Serves 4 to 6 This hearty soup is a delicious way to use the stock and tender vegetables from poaching the chicken for the Emmenthaler Chicken Breasts.

In a large soup pot, combine the vegetables and cooking liquid remaining from poaching the chicken breasts with 3 cups water, and 1 cup picked over and rinsed lentil de Puys (French lentils). Bring to a boil, lower the heat, and simmer until the lentils are tender, about 20 minutes. Preheat the broiler. Divide the soup evenly among 4 to 6 ovenproof soup bowls. Top each portion with $^1/_2$ cup croutons and $^1/_4$ cup crumbled goat cheese. Place the bowls on a sturdy baking sheet. Set under the broiler, about 4 inches from the heat source, and broil until the cheese is melted and the soup is bubbly. Serve immediately.

LAMB AND EGGPLANT GRATIN
with NORTH AFRICAN SPICES

Serves 6 to 8   With its rich layers of eggplant, spiced ground lamb, tangy feta cheese, and wal-nuts, this hearty gratin has all the flavors of a rich moussaka, the well-loved eggplant casserole of Greece—but it's much easier to make. This is one of those dishes that tastes best when made a day ahead. Top it with a dollop of creamy yogurt, if you like, and serve it with a crisp green salad made with cucumbers and a bit of dill.

1 eggplant (1¹/₂ pounds), cut into ¹/₄-inch slices

Sauce

1 pound ground lamb

1 large yellow onion, finely chopped

2 large cloves garlic, chopped

1¹/₂ tablespoons ground cumin

1 tablespoon ground cinnamon

¹/₂ teaspoon ground allspice

¹/₄ to ¹/₂ teaspoon red pepper flakes

¹/₂ to 1 teaspoon kosher salt

¹/₂ teaspoon freshly ground black pepper

1 (28-ounce) can crushed tomatoes

1 cup water

¹/₃ cup chopped fresh flat-leaf parsley

PREHEAT THE OVEN TO 350°F. Lightly oil an 8 by 11-inch (2-quart) gratin dish. Generously oil a large baking sheet with olive oil.

ARRANGE THE EGGPLANT SLICES in a single layer on the prepared baking sheet. Turn the slices over once so that both sides are lightly coated with the oil. Bake until they begin to take on some color and are soft and pliable, about 30 minutes.

TO MAKE THE SAUCE: Heat a large sauté pan over high heat. Add the lamb and cook, using a spatula to break up the lumps, until beginning to brown, about 5 minutes. Using a slotted spoon, transfer the lamb to a bowl. Drain all but 2 tablespoons of the fat from the pan. Add the onion and cook over medium-high heat until translucent, about 3 minutes. Add the garlic and cook for 1 minute. Add the cumin, cinnamon, allspice, red pepper flakes, salt, and pepper and cook until fragrant, about 1 minute. Return the lamb to the pan and stir to combine. Add the tomatoes and ¹/₂ cup of the water; bring to a boil. Lower the heat and simmer, uncovered, stirring occasionally,

continued

Topping

2 cups crumbled feta or ricotta salata cheese

$^1/_2$ cup walnuts, toasted and coarsely chopped

$^1/_2$ cup fresh bread crumbs

1 tablespoon chopped fresh flat-leaf parsley

1 tablespoon olive oil

2 tablespoons chopped fresh mint, for garnish

2 tablespoons chopped fresh cilantro, for garnish

until thickened and the flavors have melded, 5 to 10 minutes. Remove from the heat and stir in the remaining $^1/_2$ cup water and the parsley. Set aside.

TO MAKE THE TOPPING: In a medium bowl, combine the feta, walnuts, bread crumbs, and parsley; toss well. Drizzle the olive oil over the bread-crumb mixture and toss until the bread crumbs have absorbed all of the oil. Set aside.

SPREAD ABOUT 1 CUP OF THE SAUCE in the bottom of the prepared gratin dish. Arrange half of the eggplant slices over the sauce so that they are touching but not overlapping. Sprinkle 1 cup of the topping over the eggplant; cover with about 2 more cups of the sauce. Arrange the remaining eggplant slices over the sauce, again touching but not overlapping. Cover the eggplant with about 1 cup of the sauce and sprinkle the remaining topping evenly over the top.

PLACE THE GRATIN ON A STURDY BAKING SHEET. Bake until hot and bubbly and the topping is crisped and lightly browned, 20 to 30 minutes. Let rest for at least 10 minutes before serving, garnished with the mint and cilantro.

LAMB CHOP CASSOULET

Serves 4 Cassoulet is a glorious stew of beans, duck, sausage, and pork from the south of France. It is simmered slowly until the flavors are intense and the texture is rich and velvety. Some restaurants claim to have a "perpetual pot" of it simmering away, to which ingredients have been added for decades. If you love cassoulet but don't have decades to spend in the kitchen, try this easy version. If you're not partial to lamb, try it with pork chops, and substitute sage for the parsley.

4 thin lamb shoulder chops ($1^{1}/_{2}$ to 2 pounds total)

Kosher salt and freshly ground black pepper

1 yellow onion, finely chopped

2 cloves garlic, sliced

$^{3}/_{4}$ cup dry white wine

2 (15-ounce) cans cannellini beans, rinsed and drained

1 (15-ounce) can diced tomatoes

$1^{1}/_{2}$ teaspoons minced fresh rosemary

Topping

$^{1}/_{4}$ cup unsalted butter

1 cup fresh bread crumbs

$^{1}/_{4}$ cup minced fresh flat-leaf parsley

PREHEAT THE OVEN TO 350°F. Lightly oil an 8 by 11-inch (2-quart) gratin dish.

SEASON BOTH SIDES OF THE LAMB CHOPS with salt and pepper. Scatter half of the onion and half of the garlic over the bottom of the prepared gratin dish. Arrange the lamb chops in a single layer over the onion and garlic. Pour the wine evenly over the lamb and sprinkle with the remaining onion and garlic. Cover the dish tightly with aluminum foil and place on a sturdy baking sheet. Bake for 1 hour.

REMOVE THE FOIL AND STIR IN THE BEANS, tomatoes, and rosemary. Season to taste with salt and pepper. Cover and continue baking until the lamb is very tender, about 30 minutes.

MEANWHILE, MAKE THE TOPPING: In a small sauté pan, melt the butter over medium-high heat until just beginning to brown. Add the bread crumbs and cook, stirring often, until the butter has been absorbed and the bread crumbs are just beginning to brown. Remove from the heat; add the parsley and mix well.

INCREASE THE OVEN TEMPERATURE TO 450°F. Sprinkle the topping over the lamb and beans; bake uncovered until the crumb topping is crisp and golden brown, 15 to 20 minutes. Let rest for 5 minutes before serving.

DIG-IN DESSERTS

Apple Gratin à la Crème

Gratinéed Peach Melba

Gratinéed Strawberry Sabayon

Tangelo Custard Gratin

Cherry-Chocolate Crème Brûlée

Amaretti-Topped Apricot Gratin

Pear-Pecan Pound Cake Gratin

Rhubarb and Raspberry Gratin

APPLE GRATIN *à la* CRÈME

Serves 4 to 6 Apples are one of the most versatile fruits, with over 7,500 varieties to choose from for baking or eating out of hand. With so many different kinds in the store, it's often hard to decide on a variety to cook. Use firm, sweet apples such as Braeburn, Cortland, or Gala, as they contain enough acid to retain lots of flavor and enough texture that they hold together when cooked. Sprinkling the apples with Calvados—the French apple-flavored brandy of Normandy—really intensifies the apple flavor.

5 firm, sweet apples (about 3 pounds), peeled, cored, and thinly sliced

1 tablespoon cornstarch or tapioca starch

2 tablespoons Calvados or brandy

1 cup heavy cream

1 teaspoon vanilla extract

1 tablespoon sugar (optional)

Topping

1 cup fresh bread crumbs

1 cup chopped walnuts

$1/4$ to $1/3$ cup firmly packed dark brown sugar

$1/4$ cup unsalted butter, melted

PREHEAT THE OVEN TO 350°F. Generously butter a 12-inch ($1^1/_2$-quart) oval gratin dish.

IN A LARGE BOWL, COMBINE THE APPLES, cornstarch, Calvados, cream, vanilla, and sugar; toss gently to mix. Transfer the apple mixture to the prepared gratin dish. Place on a sturdy baking sheet. Bake for 30 minutes.

TO MAKE THE TOPPING: In a medium bowl, combine the bread crumbs, walnuts, and brown sugar; toss to mix. Drizzle the melted butter over the bread-crumb mixture and toss until the bread crumbs have absorbed all of the butter. Sprinkle the topping evenly over the apples. Return to the oven and bake until golden and bubbly, about 30 minutes. Let rest for 5 minutes before serving.

GRATINÉED PEACH MELBA

Serves 4 to 6 Peaches should be peeled for cooking, a chore that can be avoided by using frozen or canned; however, the flavor of ripe peaches is one of the biggest pleasures at the markets, and it shines in this gratin if fresh are available. There are two categories of peaches, cling and freestone. The clings are usually the first to arrive in season and the juiciest, but the fruit "clings" to the stone, or pit, and is difficult to remove. Freestone, as the name implies, has a stone that is free of the flesh and can be removed easily. Nectarines can be substituted in this recipe, and they don't have to be peeled.

2 or 3 large ripe peaches (about 1 pound), peeled and sliced

1 pint raspberries

$1/4$ cup Demerara or washed raw cane sugar

8 ounces mascarpone cheese

Topping

1 cup sliced almonds

1 cup crushed amaretti cookies

To ancient Greeks, peaches were known as the "golden fruit of the gods," and peach trees were among the first trees to be planted by the Spaniards in the California missions.

PREHEAT THE BROILER. Butter a 12-inch ($1^1/_2$-quart) oval gratin dish.

IN A MEDIUM BOWL, gently toss together the peaches and raspberries. Arrange the mixture in the bottom of the prepared gratin dish in an even layer. Sprinkle the sugar over the fruit, then dollop the mascarpone over the top, spreading it as much as possible with the back of a spoon.

TO MAKE THE TOPPING: In a medium bowl, combine the almonds and amaretti crumbs; toss to mix. Sprinkle the almond mixture evenly over the fruit and marscapone.

SET UNDER THE BROILER, about 4 inches from the heat source, and broil until the topping is golden, about 3 to 5 minutes—the fruit will be warmed, but not bubbling. Serve immediately.

NOTE: To peel peaches, cut an X in the blossom ends. Plunge a few at a time into a large pot of boiling water for 30 to 60 seconds. Transfer with a slotted spoon to a bowl of ice water to stop the cooking. When cool enough to handle, peel the skins using your fingers or a small, sharp knife. If the peaches are firm, they may be peeled with a serrated vegetable peeler or small, sharp knife.

GRATINÉED STRAWBERRY SABAYON

Serves 6   The French sauce called sabayon, like its Italian cousin, *zabaglione*, is a frothy custard sauce made with egg yolks, sugar, and sweet white wine. It is usually eaten as dessert, although you will see savory versions served with fish and seafood. Spooned warm over fresh strawberries in tall champagne glasses, it is creamy perfection. Take that idea one step further by giving the sabayon a dusting of sugar and lightly browning it under the broiler. Who says perfection can't be improved upon?

Sabayon

4 large egg yolks

$1/3$ cup sugar

$1/2$ cup late-harvest Riesling or other sweet white wine

$1/2$ cup heavy cream, whipped to soft peaks

2 pints ripe strawberries, hulled and sliced

2 teaspoons sugar

PREHEAT THE BROILER. Lightly butter a 12-inch ($1^1/2$-quart) oval gratin dish or six 8-ounce ramekins.

TO MAKE THIS SABAYON: In the bottom of a double boiler, bring 2 inches of water to a boil over high heat; lower the heat and maintain a simmer. In the top of the double boiler, whisk together the egg yolks, sugar, and wine. Place over, but not touching, the simmering water and beat constantly, using an electric mixer, until light and fluffy, about 10 minutes. The mixture will go from frothy and bubbly to light and fluffy. Do not overcook or the eggs will scramble. Remove the top of the double boiler from the water and continue beating until cool. Carefully fold the whipped cream into the sabayon.

ARRANGE THE STRAWBERRIES in the bottom of the prepared gratin dish(es). Spoon the sabayon evenly over the strawberries and sprinkle with the sugar. Place on a sturdy baking sheet. Set under the broiler, about 4 inches from the heat source, and broil, rotating as needed, until the sugar is lightly caramelized and golden, 1 to 2 minutes. Serve immediately.

TANGELO CUSTARD GRATIN

Serves 6 Tangelos are hybrids of mandarin oranges and grapefruit, with a tart flavor reminiscent of tangerines. Look for bright, shiny specimens that are heavy for their size. The tangy flavor of the tangelos in this gratin contrasts with the silky texture of the custard and the light crust of caramelized sugar. You can prepare the fruit and the custard up to five hours ahead and refrigerate until to ready use. Strain off any juice from the fruit before spooning over the custard. Sipping the extra juice is the cook's perk!

6 tangelos

2 cups half-and-half

1/3 cup sugar

1/4 cup cornstarch

1 large egg plus 4 egg yolks

2 tablespoons unsalted butter, at room temperature

1/2 teaspoon vanilla extract

6 tablespoons sugar

USING A VEGETABLE PEELER, remove the tangelo zest in thin strips, taking care to remove just the colored part of the peel.

IN A SMALL SAUCEPAN, bring the half-and-half just to a boil over medium-high heat. Remove from the heat, add the tangelo zest, cover, and let steep about 1 hour. Strain the half-and-half through a fine-mesh sieve and return to the pan. Discard the zest.

USING A SHARP KNIFE, remove the remaining peel from the tangelos, taking care to remove all the white pith. Holding a tangelo over a bowl, slice between the membrane and the fruit on each side of each segment, and let the freed segments drop into the bowl. Repeat with the remaining tangelos. Squeeze the membranes over the bowl to release any remaining juice.

IN A LARGE BOWL, WHISK TOGETHER THE SUGAR, cornstarch, egg, and egg yolks until the mixture becomes a light lemon yellow color, about 3 minutes. Return the half-and-half to a boil over medium-high heat. Remove from the heat and add slowly, whisking vigorously, to the egg mixture. Return the mixture to the saucepan and whisk over medium heat until the custard is thick and bubbling, 2 to 3 minutes. Remove from the heat and whisk in the butter, vanilla, and $^1/_2$ cup of the tangelo juice. Transfer the custard to a bowl and place a piece of plastic wrap directly on the surface to prevent a skin from forming. Let cool, then refrigerate until cold.

PREHEAT THE BROILER. Using a slotted spoon, remove the tangelo segments from the juice and divide evenly among six 6-ounce ramekins or shallow dishes. Drink the remaining juice or reserve for another use.

SPOON THE CUSTARD OVER THE TANGELO SEGMENTS, covering most of the fruit but leaving a few spots showing through. Sprinkle the custards with the sugar. Place the dishes on a sturdy baking sheet. Set under the broiler, about 4 inches from the heat source, and broil, rotating as needed, until the sugar is caramelized and golden, 1 to 2 minutes. (Alternatively, you can use a kitchen butane torch to caramelize the tops.) Serve immediately.

CHERRY-CHOCOLATE CRÈME BRÛLÉE

Serves 6 This dish is a variation on the traditional crème brûlée recipe said to have originated at Trinity College in Cambridge, England. The ultimate topping of a crackled crust of caramelized sugar covers the sensually sinful, silky custard flavored with dark chocolate to complement the sour cherries inside. Use a best-quality chocolate such as Callebaut, Valrhrona, or Scharffen Berger.

3 ounces bittersweet chocolate, finely chopped

3 ounces semisweet chocolate, finely chopped

8 large egg yolks

³/₄ cups sugar

3 cups heavy cream

1 teaspoon vanilla extract

1 (16-ounce) jar sour cherries in light syrup, drained and patted dry

PLACE THE BITTERSWEET AND SEMISWEET CHOCOLATES in a medium bowl and rest a fine-mesh sieve over the top.

IN A LARGE BOWL, WHISK TOGETHER THE EGG YOLKS and ¹/₄ cup of the sugar until a light lemon yellow, about 3 minutes.

IN A MEDIUM SAUCEPAN, bring the cream to a boil and immediately remove from the heat. Slowly add one-third of the hot cream, whisking constantly, to the egg yolks. Whisk the tempered egg yolk mixture into the remaining hot cream in the pan and cook, whisking gently, over medium-low heat, taking care not to allow the mixture to boil. The custard will thicken and should coat the back of a spoon. Immediately pour the custard through the sieve and onto the chopped chocolate. Stir until the chocolate has melted and the mixture is smooth. Add the vanilla.

DIVIDE THE CHERRIES EVENLY among six, 8-ounce ramekins. Pour over the chocolate custard and let cool to room temperature. Refrigerate until firm, about 4 hours.

PREHEAT THE BROILER. Place the chilled custards on a baking sheet. Sprinkle the remaining ¹/₂ cup sugar evenly over the tops. Set under the broiler, about 4 inches from the heat source, and broil until the sugar is caramelized and golden,. (Alternatively, you can use a kitchen butane torch to caramelize the tops.) Serve immediately.

AMARETTI-TOPPED APRICOT GRATIN

Serves 4 to 6 The rich custard in this gratin is flavored with a thick purée of poached dried apricots and topped with a crisp layer of sliced almonds and almond-flavored cookies. Use the flavorful, dark orange Californian varieties of apricots, with their naturally tart flavor, rather than the mild, plumped yellow kind, often sold as snacks. Amaretti are little, airy, crunchy Italian almond macaroon cookies, available in specialty food stores.

12 ounces dried apricots

2 cups water

2 cups half-and-half

3 large eggs

3 tablespoons sugar

2 tablespoons freshly squeezed lemon juice

1 teaspoon vanilla extract

Topping

1/2 cup crushed amaretti cookies

1/4 cup sliced almonds

2 tablespoons unsalted butter, melted

IN A BOWL, COMBINE THE APRICOTS with the water; let soak until soft, about 2 hours.

PREHEAT THE OVEN TO 325°F. Transfer the softened apricots and the soaking liquid to a saucepan and bring to a boil over high heat. Lower the heat and simmer until the apricots are very tender, about 10 minutes.

TRANSFER THE POACHED APRICOTS and 1 cup of the cooking liquid to a blender and purée until very smooth. It should be the consistency of heavy cream; if it is too thick, add a little more of the cooking liquid. Add the half-and-half, eggs, sugar, lemon juice, and vanilla and purée until very smooth. Divide the mixture evenly among four to six, 6- or 8-ounce ramekins.

TO MAKE THE TOPPING: In a small bowl, combine the crushed amaretti and almonds. Drizzle the butter over the cookie-crumb mixture and toss until the cookie crumbs have absorbed all of the butter.

TO SERVE THE CUSTARDS HOT: Sprinkle the topping evenly over the tops of the custards. Place the ramekins in a large baking dish and add enough boiling water to come about halfway up the sides of the individual dishes. Bake until just set and the topping is golden, about 30 minutes. They will continue to firm up as they cool, so don't overcook the custards. Serve immediately.

TO SERVE THE CUSTARDS COLD: Place the ramekins in a large baking dish and add enough boiling water to come about halfway up the sides of the individual dishes. Bake until just set, about 30 minutes. They will continue to firm up as they cool, so don't overcook the custards. Let cool to room temperature; cover with plastic wrap and refrigerate for 4 hours or up to overnight. When ready to serve, preheat the broiler. Sprinkle the topping evenly over the custards and place the ramekins on a sturdy baking sheet. Set under the broiler, about 4 inches from the heat source, and broil until golden and crispy, about 3 minutes. Serve immediately.

PEAR-PECAN POUND CAKE GRATIN

Serves 4   Pears are one of the few fruits that can be successfully purchased unripe and ripened at home, so don't pass up attractive displays of these famously shaped fruits just because they feel very hard. For this recipe, use firm but ripe Bosc or Bartlett pears and cut them into cubes so that they hold their shape during cooking. You can include some raspberries, if you like, to add a tart flavor to the dish; just sprinkle them over the cooked pears immediately before the topping is added.

1$^1/_2$ pounds ripe pears, peeled, cored, and cut into $^1/_2$-inch dice

Juice of 1 lemon

2 teaspoons instant tapioca

Topping

$^1/_4$ pound pound cake, cut into $^1/_2$-inch cubes

1 tablespoon unsalted butter, melted

$^1/_2$ cup chopped pecans

$^1/_2$ cup chocolate chips

4 teaspoons Demerara or washed raw cane sugar

Whipped cream, for garnish

PREHEAT THE OVEN TO 350°F. Generously butter four, 8-ounce ramekins; set aside.

TO MAKE THE FILLING: In a medium bowl, combine the pears, lemon juice, and tapioca; toss gently to mix. Divide the pears evenly among the prepared dishes.

TO MAKE THE TOPPING: In a medium bowl, drizzle the pound cake with the melted butter; toss gently to coat. Add the pecans and chocolate chips; toss gently to mix. Divide the topping among the dishes, pressing down just a bit to fit it into the dish. Sprinkle 1 teaspoon of the sugar over each gratin.

PLACE THE RAMEKINS ON A STURDY BAKING SHEET. Bake until golden and bubbly, about 30 minutes. Let rest for 10 minutes before serving. Serve dolloped with whipped cream.

RHUBARB *and* RASPBERRY GRATIN

Serves 4 to 6 Easy is the name of the game in this gratin—and the topping can be used universally as the topping for any fruit gratin. The tart rhubarb-raspberry filling contrasts with the fragrant cinnamon and toasty hazelnuts. Try it on top of fresh apricots or a combination of blackberries and apple, or just sprinkle the topping over some leftover cooked fruit. Rhubarb is in season in the spring and can be mouth puckering, so adjust the amount of sugar to your taste.

1¹/₂ pounds rhubarb, cut into 1-inch pieces

1¹/₂ pints fresh raspberries, or 1 (12-ounce) package frozen raspberries, thawed

¹/₃ to ³/₄ cup granulated sugar

Topping

2 cups fresh bread crumbs

¹/₂ cup chopped hazelnuts

3 tablespoons Demerara or other washed raw sugar

1 teaspoon ground cinnamon

¹/₄ cup unsalted butter, melted

Softly whipped cream or vanilla ice cream, for serving

PREHEAT THE OVEN TO 350°F. Combine the rhubarb, raspberries, and ¹/₃ cup of the granulated sugar in a 7 by 9-inch (1-quart) gratin dish.

PLACE THE GRATIN ON A STURDY BAKING SHEET. Bake until the rhubarb is tender when pierced with the tip of a knife and there are lots of juices bubbling in the pan, about 45 minutes. At this point, taste and adjust the sugar if needed.

TO MAKE THE TOPPING: in a medium bowl, combine the bread crumbs, hazelnuts, 2 tablespoons of the Demerara sugar, and the cinnamon. Drizzle the butter over the bread-crumb mixture and toss until the bread-crumbs have absorbed all of the butter; set aside.

SPRINKLE THE BREAD CRUMB MIXTURE EVENLY over the top of the gratin and sprinkle with the remaining tablespoon of Demerara sugar. Bake until golden, about 30 minutes. Let rest for 5 minutes before serving.

SERVE HOT, WARM, OR COLD with a dollop of softly whipped cream or a scoop of vanilla ice cream.

RESOURCES

All-Clad
424 Morganza Road
Canonsburg, Pennsylvania 15317
800-255-2523
www.all-clad.com

The Baker's Catalogue
King Arthur Flour Company
P.O. Box 876
Norwich, Vermont 05055-0876
800-827-6836
www.bakerscatalogue.com

Chef's Catalog
P.O. Box 620048
Dallas, Texas 75262-0048
800-338-3232
www.chefscatalog.com

Dean and Deluca
2526 East 36th Street, North Circle
Wichita, Kansas 67219
877-826-9246
www.deananddeluca.com

Emile Henry
www.emilehenry.com

HomeChef
www.homechef.com

Kitchen Aid
800-541-6390
www.kitchenaid.com

Le Creuset
877-273-8738
www.lecreuset.com

J.B. Prince Company
36 East 31st Street
New York, New York 10016
800-473-0577
www.jbprince.com

Professional Cutlery Direct
242 Branford Road
North Branford, Connecticut 06471
www.cutlery.com

Staub
www.staubusa.com

Sur La Table
Catalog Division
P.O. Box 34707
Seattle, Washington 98124
800-243-0852
www.surlatable.com

Viking Range Corporation
111 Front Street
Greenwood, Mississippi 38930
622-455-1200
www.vikingrange.com

Williams-Sonoma
Mail Order Department
P.O. Box 37990
Las Vegas, Nevada 89137
800-541-2233
www.williams-sonoma.com

TABLE Of EQUIVALENTS

VOLUME MEASURES

U.S.		METRIC		IMPERIAL	
$^1/_2$	teaspoon	2.5	milliliters		
1	teaspoon	5	milliliters		
1	tablespoon	15	milliliters	1	fluid ounce
$^1/_4$	cup	60	milliliters	2	fluid ounces
$^1/_3$	cup	75	milliliters	$2^1/_2$	fluid ounces
$^1/_2$	cup	125	milliliters	4	fluid ounces
1	cup	250	milliliters	8	fluid ounces
2	cups (1 pint)	500	milliliters	16	fluid ounces
4	cups (1 quart)	1000	milliliters	32	fluid ounces

WEIGHT MEASURES

U.S.		METRIC	
1	ounce	28	grams
4	ounces	112	grams
8	ounces	224	grams
1	pound	448	grams
2.2	pounds	1	kilogram

OVEN TEMPERATURES

FAHRENHEIT	CELSIUS	GAS
225	110	$^1/_4$
250	120	$^1/_2$
275	140	1
300	150	2
325	160	3
350	180	4
375	190	5
400	200	6
425	220	7
450	230	8
475	240	9